MW00533354

ELLIOTT CLARK FOUNDER OF APARTMENT BARTENDER

LET'S DO DRINKS

**INSPIRATIONAL TIPS, PERSONAL SECRETS AND
75+ RECIPES FOR A FANCY NIGHT OUT WITHOUT LEAVING THE HOUSE**

PHOTOGRAPHY BY ELLIOTT CLARK & SHAWN CAMPBELL

TABLE OF CONTENTS

29

104

234

FOREWORD

The first time I met Elliott Clark wasn't at a bartending competition, industry event or glitzy brand trip—it was on the side of a street, in front of a dusty construction site on a brutally hot Colorado afternoon. I handed him a hard hat and we exchanged some pleasantries before creeping through a break in the chain-link fence and venturing into what would become Death & Co Denver.

Elliott asked questions. Not just about the shiny stuff—the grandeur of the space, the techniques behind every drink—but about the philosophy of what we wanted to bring to Denver. He asked about the cocktails, sure, but in a nuanced way, with the kind of detail only a true student of the craft would have. I had a sense that beneath his clear talent for photography and creating social media content that resonated with followers, there was a deeper passion, the kind of obsessiveness that comes with finding the thing you love most in the world. I immediately felt a kinship. We continued to collaborate with Elliott over the next few months, him capturing the opening training and, to our great benefit, shooting the first moments that the lights dimmed at Death & Co Denver. He was there for every step, clearly as excited as everyone on the team for the doors to open.

The thing about working with talented people is they'll inspire you in the most unexpected ways. After those first months of working together, Elliott's final photos of the finished space hit my inbox. There's one that has stuck with me to this day: the shot is framed like a shotgun down the room, the bar's dramatic arches towering in the background, the foreground scattered with leather chairs and vintage rugs, our massive crystal chandeliers hanging like angelic sentries from the ceiling. The image is dripping in opulence. I couldn't stop looking at it (I still can't). It's full of emotion and potential energy, a room in repose but fearlessly self-confident and exactly where you want to spend all your time. I had spent years planning that space and helping bring

A view of Death & Co Denver taken by Elliott Clark and cherished by Alex Day.

it to life—hell, I was standing next to him when the photo was taken!—but in that moment, I saw our bar as the idealized version of itself. I vowed to make Death & Co live up to the expectations captured in the image. His art, in that moment, shaped my art.

In the pages that follow, Elliott will similarly change your relationship with cocktails. His passion for drinks and entertaining is clear, as is his commitment to sharing what he's discovered to help you make drinks at home the best they can be and share them with others. From a foundation of necessary tools and ingredients, Let's Do Drinks helpfully sets the tone with the classics—indispensable in their universal appeal and the building blocks for your own cocktail creativity. From here, he opens the door to his (and some friends') processes with a collection of delicious drinks that are perfect for any occasion.

You'll discover instruction subtly hiding in every corner of the book. After years of capturing the world's best bartenders (and no doubt asking them thoughtful questions), Elliott has a way of capturing more than just a drink in repose. Each photo tells a story and will hopefully provoke you to try something new, to refine your craft. Witness the float technique captured in the Masala Chai Sour (pg. 232), the bar spoon inverted and hovering at the perfect distance above the glass. Or the flamed orange twist on the Añejo Nightcap (pg. 216), showing the just-right placement of the peel next to a flame (don't let them touch!). Observe the simple but beautiful garnish on the Whiskey Sour (pg. 116), something that can be prepped before your guests arrive and will elevate your game immediately.

Despite years of bartending and having penned three books on cocktails, I don't often make cocktails at home. When I do, they're hilariously simple—a batched martini in the freezer, some impromptu post-dinner Negronis or, in rare moments of inspiration, a giant pitcher of palomas (taco night!). As I read Let's Do Drinks, I felt not only a reigniting of my love of cocktails but also a call to action to bring them back into my personal life. Be it a quiet night on the couch or a gathering with friends and family, Elliott reminds us again and again that cocktails are not singular creations to be enjoyed in isolation (though they can be!). Rather, they are vessels for deeper human connection. Let's do drinks.

ALEX DAY

Partner, Death & Co
Author, Death & Co: Modern Classic Cocktails;
Cocktail Codex: Fundamentals, Formulas, Evolutions;
Death & Co: Welcome Home

INTRODUCTION

April 9, 2015, was the day I accidentally fell in love.

I was a recent college graduate with the cliché idea that I needed to figure out what I wanted to do with the rest of my life. I was working a 9 to 5 job for a tech company cold calling dead leads ("Smile and dial," as they say). As you'd imagine, I desperately wanted to do something else, but I didn't know what. I was craving something that wouldn't have me stuck in a chair for 10 hours staring at a computer screen. Something creative. Something useful.

I often took weekend trips to escape reality. One such trip took me to New York City to visit a lifelong friend and his wife. They were newly married, and one of their wedding presents was a Cocktails 101 class in Manhattan. It happened to be the day I arrived in town, so naturally I got an invite. Free drinks? Count me in.

Upon arriving, we were handed a welcome drink, which I excitedly sipped. The drink was bright red and bitter as hell. I whispered to my friend, "This tastes like shit." That was my first time tasting a negroni (I later learned it was my palate that sucked, not the drink).

My first guest
bartending pop-up at
tiki bar Lost Lake in
Chicago, Illinois, 2017.

Top row from left: The Cocktails 101 class in New York City, where it all started, 2015; Cohosting a special cobranded cocktail menu launch event with Hilton Hotels, 2019.

Middle row from left: Shaking up cocktails on camera at a wine and spirits convention, 2018; Sipping old fashioneds at Billy Sunday in Chicago, Illinois, 2019.

Bottom row from left: Speaking at a seminar in Berlin on future drink trends, 2018; Doing a guest bartending pop-up at The Blind Rabbit, a speakeasy in Anaheim, California, 2019.

In that class, we learned how to build a cocktail. When to shake and when to stir. The difference between spirits, liqueurs and bitters. Then we were challenged to put that knowledge to the test by crafting our own custom beverage. The experiment was on. I loaded a cocktail shaker with vodka, simple syrup, lemon wedges, strawberries, blueberries and mint leaves. I muddled the ingredients, shook them with ice and strained the drink into a coupe glass. This was the first drink I ever made from scratch. It had a nice red hue with pulp, mint and berry pieces floating on top. No, it wasn't the prettiest cocktail, but it didn't taste half bad considering I didn't know what the hell I was doing. It was a light bulb moment for me. This was the creative outlet I was looking for. I just had to figure out how to do it.

It wasn't just one thing that made me feel this way. It was a cocktail of moments. It was being there with my friends, sitting in that kitchen with 10 strangers gathered together, laughing and conversing like we'd been acquainted for years, learning something new. It was the creative process of making a cocktail; layering spirits, fresh ingredients and different flavors on top of each other to create something delicious. To say that Cocktails 101 class changed my life is an understatement, because here I am nearly a decade later writing a book about making drinks.

After that trip to New York, I returned home to my apartment in Phoenix inspired to continue exploring this newfound passion. I wanted to create that same feeling I had in the class, just at home.

I went to the liquor store and purchased a bunch of bottles I knew nothing about. I bought a cocktail book, then picked up a very clunky light wood bar cart

> *"I shared my journey and enthusiasm for home bartending with anybody who cared to follow along."*

from Craigslist and got to mixing. My roommate at the time would drink anything and everything you put in front of him, making him the perfect guinea pig for my creative pursuits.

Since I figured it would be a good idea to keep a visual log of the recipes I crafted for easy reference, I began taking photos of the drinks I made on a little side table near the only window in the apartment. I created an anonymous Instagram account to post the drinks I made at home for the roomie and any friends that came over. I called it Apartment Bartender.

The name started as a joke. After indulging in one too many negronis (I learned to love them) with friends one evening, I rambled on about my new hobby. "I don't know why I call myself a home bartender," I told them. "I live in a shitty apartment." Without missing a beat, my friend corrected me and said, "You're an apartment bartender." The rest, as they say, is history.

Over the next year, I got better at making drinks and even better at taking photos. I read every cocktail book I could find. I frequented my city's best cocktail bars and researched drink ingredients just for fun. I developed friendships with the bar staff and photographed menu development sessions, which gave me the chance to learn how great bartenders create unforgettable drinks. I shared my journey and enthusiasm for home bartending with anybody who cared to follow along. The little Instagram account I started just to keep a log of my recipes grew organically, so much so that I was able to quit my day job and leave cold calling behind.

It's emotional recounting all that transpired after starting Apartment Bartender because it's more than a social media account. It was my real life documented in delicious drinks. For every great moment I shared, there were hundreds of others I didn't that meant just as much. I met my closest friends on this journey. I met the person I love and started a family.

The barrel aging room at Old Forester Bourbon Distillery in Kentucky, 2022.

Apartment Bartender garnered the attention of major media outlets, the world's biggest brands and hundreds of thousands of people all over the world—all of whom cared about learning to make great drinks at home. By starting this journey, I inadvertently became one of the world's most notable home bartenders. I turned Apartment Bartender into an award-winning blog about drinks and gained recognition for the content I was creating and sharing. I led workshops and seminars on the topic for global spirit conglomerates. When one journalist called me the "founding father of the photogenic cocktail movement"—well, that was quite the brandied cherry on top.

I also traveled. A lot. Instead of shooting Manhattans or drinking daiquiris in my apartment, I was zipping all over the world. One article said my life resembled "that of a Fortune 500 CEO. Rarely in the same city for more than two days, much less the same time zone." Long gone were the days of tucking myself behind a desk for hours on end. I visited all kinds of distilleries, from the big ones we all know to obscure craft operations tucked away in remote locations. I pulled whiskey older than I was from oak barrels and sipped while learning from renowned master distillers. I planted agave and pressed my hands to the dirt mounds in Oaxaca and felt the heat from the piñas roasting below. I chewed on fresh sugarcane in Martinique before it got pressed, fermented, distilled and aged into the agricultural-style rum I love best in a daiquiri. Getting to meet the people behind the spirits we enjoy and witnessing every part of the production process made me appreciate what I was doing so much more. It also made me feel like a bit of an impostor.

"To me, home is as much about the people as the place itself."

Despite hosting pop-ups and making drinks at some of the best bars in the country, I knew I still had a lot to learn. In spite of being selected to judge the world's biggest bartending competition, Diageo World Class, a few times over (as well as a bartending throw down between Vanilla Ice and Ice T), I knew there was more I could do to further establish myself in the industry. I've made negronis on a volcano in Patagonia. I met Canelo at a barrel-aging center in Cognac. I poured fresh gimlets on a speedboat in Baja, as gray whales breached the surface all around us. I loved every moment of these incredible experiences. But part of me still wanted to be back in my apartment. Or, more precisely, back home.

To me, home is as much about the people as the place itself. I've spent numerous nights in some of the world's most celebrated cocktail bars, but I can say without hyperbole that some of the best drinks I've ever had were shaken or stirred in the comfort of my home. And it's not because of the recipe.

For me, crafting cocktails is a form of art and self-expression, a way to put a bit of myself forward for others to consider. But the people I get to enjoy that drink with are equally important. They're the reason I'm doing it! I believe a great drink has the ability to bring people together and create community. A drink on its own is just a drink, but when you add a spirit of hospitality—of graciousness and a desire to elevate—you're crafting something with care and creating moments of connection. It's what turns a sip into a story.

My goal has always been to make drinks at home feel inviting, approachable and sophisticated rather than pretentious. In the same way that Cocktails 101 course sent me down the rabbit hole, I hope this book delivers you to a wonderland of great moments. I hope it encourages you to embrace the art of slowing down and crafting something special for the people you welcome into your home. I want your friends to prefer your place over going out because they feel at peace there. I want you to feel empowered to know your own home can feel like the cocktail bar you love going to so much.

Pour yourself a drink, relax and let's dive in.

Stirring up cocktails
for friends in the
apartment, 2020.

Work with the space you have and get creative with your storage options.

THE ART OF
HOME BARTENDING

Home (or Apartment) Bartending Basics

As magical as that Cocktails 101 class was, the process of learning how to make drinks felt awkward. Prior to that day, the fanciest I got was topping vodka with some soda water and squeezing in a splash of lime juice for some added pizzazz. Clearly, I could do better.

I became mesmerized with the process of making drinks: I'd visit loungy cocktail bars like Billy Sunday in Chicago and watch the bartenders measuring liquid ingredients, stirring cocktails with ease, chipping away at large, clear blocks of ice and resting a neat chunk in a cocktail glass before pouring the drink on top. Everything just looked so damn cool to me, and I wanted to do that at home. But I didn't know where to begin.

If you're just starting out, I wish I could tell you that you'll effortlessly bypass the awkwardness of learning how to make drinks, but I'd be doing you a disservice. It's going to feel a little silly trying to stir a cocktail properly for the first time. You may learn what it's like to have the top of a cocktail shaker pop open mid-shake and feel its contents splash all over you. Consider it a baptism of sorts—a rite of passage. You're going to make a mess. Citrus juice gets all over the counter (and fruit flies love this). Homemade syrups magically affix themselves to surfaces you aren't even sure you've touched. Glassware quickly piles up in the sink after a fun night with friends and sometimes it doesn't even make it that far into the evening because gravity wins. Despite your best intentions, you will inevitably make bad drinks. Some flavor combinations only mix well in your head and have no business being combined in a glass, no matter what you do. The good news: It's all part of the process.

In the beginning, learning how to make drinks can feel like a blow to the ego. That's because it is. You're learning, so embrace the cringe. Maybe you're venturing out of your vodka soda phase or searching for a creative outlet, like I was. Maybe you're an avid home entertainer that just needs a few good drink recipes

up your sleeve. Wherever you find yourself, you're in the right place.

The awkward phase doesn't last forever, and the process of making drinks is actually quite simple. Once you understand the flow of things, it's smooth sailing.

It's best to attack the beginning stages of learning how to make drinks at home with a series of questions. Below are the questions I get asked most often, which is why I plan to answer them in the pages that follow:

- **What bar tools do I need?**
- **What bottles should I buy?**
- **What glassware do I need?**
- **Does ice matter?**
- **Should I buy syrups or make my own?**
- **How should I style my home bar?**
- **How do I make a drink?**

Other questions may arise along the way, and I urge you to seek out the answers if you don't find them in this book.

If you consider yourself a cocktail nerd with all the tools, experience and understanding of how to make drinks, then by all means, skip this section and get straight to the recipes. However, if this is your Cocktails 101 class moment, then let's dive into the questions above so you're well on your way to knowing how to make drinks.

After this, all that's left is to do it.

What Bar Tools Do I Need?

In the pursuit of honing your drink-making skills, equipping yourself with the appropriate tools can simplify your journey a great deal. Yes, it's possible to use a mason jar for a cocktail shaker or that cute little shot glass you bought in Mexico as a jigger. You could even muddle ingredients with the flat side of a cooking spoon— ultimately, you should use what you've got on hand. But if you had to choose between using the bottom of your shoe or a hammer to drive in a nail, I think we can agree the hammer wins out. The right tools make all the difference.

There are tools that are must-haves, and there are tools that are nice-to-haves depending on your budget and the space you're willing to take up in your home. Even if you live in a shitty apartment like I used to, take heart: The must-haves are small and barely take up any room.

MUST-HAVES

COCKTAIL SHAKER

There are two primary types of cocktail shaker: the Boston shaker and the cobbler shaker.

A Boston shaker (also called shaker tins) consists of two pieces—a large tin and a small tin. You'll see most bartenders using these for their speed, durability and volume, which helps when building multiple drinks at the same time.

A cobbler shaker is a three-piece set with a built-in strainer attached to the top. They tend to be more aesthetically pleasing than the Boston shaker, and are perfect when pace is a concern.

Personally, I find value in using both. When hosting larger events where you prioritize efficiency and durability, a Boston shaker is the go-to option. However, for casual gatherings at home with friends where time is not of the essence, I find myself reaching for a cobbler shaker more frequently.

Boston shaker.

Cobbler shaker.

JIGGER

This tool is used to measure liquid ingredients. Despite its critical role in crafting cocktails, the humble jigger is by far one of the most underrated and underutilized bar tools at home. Always use a jigger if you want consistency in your recipes. Jiggers typically feature dual-sided compartments. Personally, I prefer either a bell jigger or a Japanese jigger. These provide a 1-ounce measurement on one end and a 2-ounce on the other. Furthermore, these jiggers often feature incremental markings on the inside, allowing for precise measurements including ¼, ½, ¾ and 1½ ounces. Embrace the reliability and precision of a quality jigger. Creating a well-balanced drink is much easier to do when you aren't eyeballing measurements.

From left, two Japanese-style jiggers and two bell jiggers.

BAR SPOON

A bar spoon is a long, slender spoon with a spiral design that's used to stir cocktails. Its unique shape allows for a smoother stir—it won't jostle the ice, creating more dilution than you want. Nobody likes a watered-down cocktail. You can also use a bar spoon to layer drinks—simply pour a liquid slowly over the back of the spoon to create layers in the glass.

MIXING GLASS

This is a must-have for stirred cocktails and it shines on a bar cart. Improvisers take note: A pint glass is a good alternative.

STRAINER

This handy tool prevents solid ingredients from entering your drink while pouring. There are three main types of strainers: Hawthorne, julep and fine mesh.

Hawthorne strainers are commonly used with Boston shakers. They feature a spiral-shaped gate that holds back solid ingredients. If you can only have one, this is the one I'd go with.

Julep strainers are best suited for fitting mixing glasses (or pint glasses) and are exclusively used for stirred cocktails.

Fine mesh strainers act as an additional filter for shaken cocktails. When making drinks with muddled fruit or egg, fine-strain the cocktails to catch tiny pieces of fruit, mint, seeds, ice shards or even eggshells that might otherwise make their way into your glass.

Hawthorne strainer.

Julep strainer.

Fine mesh strainer.

Y-PEELER OR PARING KNIFE

Both of these tools serve as easy, efficient choices for creating citrus peels to garnish your drink with. However, pay attention and exercise caution to avoid injury.

ICE MOLD

Purchase a silicone ice mold that yields cubed ice or large clear ice—don't go the cheap route and rely on the weirdly shaped, cloudy ice that freezers typically produce on their own. That type of ice tends to melt quickly, so it will dilute (aka ruin) a well-made cocktail faster than you'd think. Clear ice from good molds doesn't just look great in a drink—it'll melt at a slower pace so your drink stays consistent as you sip. Ice molds are cost-effective and compact enough to fit in small freezer spaces, so stock up.

WINE OPENER AND BOTTLE OPENER

My go-to is a wine key that allows you to open both beer and wine, because they're compact, inexpensive and durable. However, you can go with a twist corkscrew, electric wine opener or, if you have the skill, use the side of a bartop to open a bottle of beer. Choose your own adventure.

CITRUS PRESS

Also calleda hand juicer, a citrus press extracts juice from lemons, limes and oranges. You can juice citrus by hand, but a citrus press is cheap, convenient, easy to use and requires minimal storage space, so be sure to get one.

MUDDLER

Used to press down on ingredients such as fruit and herbs to release juice, flavor and aroma. Sure, you can use a spoon, but the real thing will save you time and discomfort.

NICE-TO-HAVES

JUICER

It's easier than ever to source a quality countertop juicer for fruits like pineapples, cucumbers and apples, as well as a range of vegetables. Incorporating fresh juice into your cocktails and homemade syrups makes for the tastiest drinks. I can't recommend a juicer enough. It's worth the space.

BLENDER

Chances are you already have one of these, which is key when it comes to making frozen summer cocktails. It'll go a long way for batched margaritas (which are worth going the long way for).

LEWIS BAG AND MALLET

A canvas ice bag used to crush your own ice for drinks like a mint julep, rum swizzle or whiskey smash. If this is too much of a splurge, don't be afraid to hit up a fast food spot like Sonic and grab a cooler of pellet ice before a big event.

SMALL CULINARY TORCH

I use this tool all the time for creating elevated garnishes. They are a dream for tasks like brûléeing sugar or lightly torching the tip of a cinnamon stick or rosemary sprig to create an aromatic trail of smoke as part of the finishing touches. You can also use this to light various types of wood chips to smoke a rocks glass when making a smoked old fashioned.

What Bottles Should I Buy?

A brief overview of the major spirit categories.

WHISKEY

I can't tell you how many times I've heard someone say, "I hate whiskey, but I love bourbon!" to which I scratch my head then politely let them know that bourbon is a type of whiskey. Whiskey is a beautiful and diverse spirit and is, in my opinion, the nerdiest spirit category in the world. Whiskey can be sweet, spicy and mellow to the taste or overproof, smokey and with notes of old rubber tire. There's a flavor profile out there for every palate.

MADE FROM: Grains like barley, corn, rye and wheat

PRODUCED IN: Countries all over the world, including Scotland, the U.S., Canada, Ireland and Japan

HOW TO ENJOY IT: Neat, on ice or in cocktails like the old fashioned, Manhattan, Rob Roy, whiskey sour, mint julep, penicillin and more

HOW IT'S MADE: Technically, all whiskey begins its life as beer. The grains are first mashed and fermented with yeast, which converts the sugars into alcohol. The mixture is then distilled to increase the alcohol content and create a more concentrated flavor. Like all spirits, whiskey is clear when it is first distilled, but what gives its signature brown color is the wood barrel in which it rests as part of the aging process. The type of barrel used and length of the aging process impacts the taste, flavor and cost.

Scotch, Scotch, Scotch

Whiskey originated in Scotland and is divided into five distinct categories: single malt, single grain, blended Scotch, blended malt and blended grain. The flavor profiles of scotch whiskey tend to vary based on the region of production. The various regions in Scotland known for whisky production are Speyside, Highlands, Lowlands, Campbeltown and Islay (pronounced eye-luh).

The distillation room at Talisker, located on the Isle of Skye in Scotland.

DID YOU KNOW?

Because bourbon must be aged in new oak barrels, after the aging process is complete, many distillers sell their used bourbon barrels to vintners, brewers or even furniture makers.

Whiskey pairs well with multiple mixers, but sometimes you just want a little whiskey on the rocks.

A brandy snifter is a nice-to-have—unless you fall in love with the spirit, then it's a must.

BRANDY

I probably shouldn't play favorites, but brandy is what I enjoy most. If you're a whiskey lover, brandy makes for an amazing alternative, swapping grain for grape.

MADE FROM: Fruit juice (e.g., grape, apple, peach, pear, plum and cherry)

PRODUCED IN: Most wine-producing countries, but commonly made in France, the U.S. (particularly in California), Spain, Portugal, Mexico, South Africa, numerous South American countries

HOW TO ENJOY IT: Neat, on ice, as an ingredient in cooking or in many classic cocktails like the sidecar, Sazerac, pisco sour, milk punch and brandy Alexander

HOW IT'S MADE: After the fruit juice has been fermented and turned into wine, it is distilled to increase the alcohol content. The resulting liquid is called eau de vie ("water of life"). It's clear, potent and packs a very distinct fruity aroma and flavor profile. In some cases, the brandy is bottled right away without aging— for example, pisco, a type of grape-based brandy produced in South America, typically comes unaged. Other brandy is aged in oak barrels for several years, then blended with more mature brandy to create the final product. Like whiskey, the aging process significantly enhances the flavor and color of the spirit.

DID YOU KNOW?

French brandies (such as Cognac, Armagnac and Calvados) are among the most popular and are named after the regions in which they originate. As popular as tequila and mezcal are in Mexico, brandy is among the country's top-produced and top-selling spirits.

Bon Voyage... à Cognac

I visited the region of Cognac early in my Apartment Bartender journey. At the time, I didn't know anything about brandy as a spirit, so getting the chance to experience the big Cognac-producing houses (e.g., Remy Martin, Hennessy, Martell) as well as small family producers really opened my eyes to how elegant and beautiful this spirit is. I walked through cellars lined with barrels that were centuries old—it felt like a walk through time.

A Note on Cognac

There are indicators on bottles produced in Cognac that denote the length of the aging process. Other regions have similar designations, with slightly different age spans.

- VS (very special): aged for a minimum of two years
- VSOP (very superior old pale): aged for a minimum of four years
- XO (extra old): aged for a minimum of 10 years

Brandy aging in large oak vats in Cognac.

GIN

Gin is an amazing spirit full of botanicals, flavor and complexities that come out with every sip. The creation process is not dissimilar from making tea—you're effectively steeping the distilled spirit with various natural ingredients to achieve a particular flavor. It's incredibly versatile as well as varied, since most gins use a proprietary blend of ingredients. It's great for spirit-forward cocktails as well as floral citrusy drinks during the warmer months.

MADE FROM: A neutral spirit typically derived from grains (like rye, barley or wheat) and distilled with juniper berries and other botanicals (dried herbs, bark, roots and citrus peels)

PRODUCED IN: Countries all over the world, but originally in the Netherlands as "genever"

HOW TO ENJOY IT: Neat, or most commonly in classic cocktails like the gin and tonic, Negroni, Tom Collins and gimlet

HOW IT'S MADE: The original grain spirit is distilled with juniper berries (because in order to be called a gin, a predominant flavor of juniper is necessary). Beyond this,

Beyond Basic

Other common styles of gin include Plymouth gin (which is also a brand), navy strength (which tends to be overproof) and Old Tom gin (which is a sweeter cordial-style gin).

gin is distilled in a number of methods and with a wide array of other botanicals like dried herbs, roots or citrus peels. The combination of botanicals varies depending on the producer and style of gin they're going for—it can be floral, bitter, citrusy, spicy, aromatic or dry. After the gin is steeped, it is redistilled and bottled. Gin is rarely aged in barrels, though it can be (and is delicious).

DID YOU KNOW?

The most common type of gin you'll find is London dry, characterized by a clean, crisp juniper-forward flavor.

Neutral spirit flows into a vat full of aromatics and botanicals.

Copper pot stills at the Sipsmith Gin distillery in London. Copper plays an essential role with gin, influencing its flavor.

Gin comes in a range of flavor profiles and botanicals. Best to try a few.

A mezcalero I met during my trip to Oaxaca enjoying the fruits of his labor.

MEZCAL

Mezcal, an artisanal and complex spirit with roots in ancient Mexican tradition, makes for some of the best drinking experiences. Despite its historical significance, I still consider it to be an emerging spirit, with so much more to learn and taste about it as it gains more and more distribution around the world.

MADE FROM: The agave plant

PRODUCED IN: Mexican states such as Oaxaca, Guerrero, Durango and San Luis Potosi

HOW TO ENJOY IT: Neat in a small cup called a copita with a slice of orange and side of worm salt or in traditional tequila cocktails like a margarita, paloma or even old fashioned variations like the Oaxacan old fashioned. I rarely sip mezcal with ice— it's best at room temperature to experience the full flavor.

A copita ("little cup") is the traditional vessel to serve mezcal.

HOW IT'S MADE: Harvested agave plants have their leaves removed to expose the heart of the plant, aka the piña. The piñas are then roasted in underground pit ovens, imparting the distinct smoky flavor that mezcal is known for. (It's worth noting that not all mezcal varieties have a smoky flavor profile, but most do.) This roasting process prepares the plant's sugars to be converted into alcohol. The softened piñas are crushed to extract their juices, traditionally done using a large stone wheel called a tahona. The extracted juice is fermented and distilled multiple times to create a clear and strong spirit. Mezcal can be aged in barrels to create a reposado and añejo expression, though it's not typical.

DID YOU KNOW?

Unlike tequila, which is made exclusively from one type of agave, mezcal offers a wide range of flavors by using various agave species. There are more than 200 known species of agave plant, and mezcal can be made from 30 or more types of agave, each contributing its own distinct characteristics.

A Trip to Oaxaca

I had the opportunity to experience the mezcal production process in Oaxaca firsthand. Agave plants are carefully grown and harvested, a process which can take anywhere from seven to 20 years, depending on the species. The most common variety, called Espadín, is widely used due to its high sugar content and relatively quick maturation. Other agave plants producing mezcal worth knowing are tobalá, tepeztate, tobaziche and arroqueño. A quality bottle of mezcal should tell you where it's from, who produced it and the agave species (typically, the more information you see on the bottle, the better the contents are).

On location in Oaxaca—easily one of my favorite "work trips."

TEQUILA

A beautiful spirit with a rich history, tequila is the foundation for some of the best classic cocktails. It is also, more than any other spirit, the one I hear people recounting negative experiences with. Overconsumption of any spirit will lead to a bad experience, so if you count yourself among the "If I drink tequila I'll go crazy" crowd, I recommend giving quality tequila a chance to change the narrative.

MADE FROM: The blue weber agave plant

PRODUCED IN: Mexico, specifically Guanajuato, Michoacan, Nayarit, Tamaulipas and Jalisco

HOW TO ENJOY IT: Neat, on ice or in many classic drinks such as a margarita, paloma, Bloody Maria, tequila sunrise and many more

HOW IT'S MADE: After blue weber agave is farmed and harvested, its leaves are cut off using a traditional tool called a coa. The piñas are then baked, and the juice is extracted before this sugary liquid is fermented with yeast, turning it into alcohol. Once fermentation is finished, the liquid is heated and distilled in large stills, separating out impurities and creating a clear, potent liquid. Tequila is typically distilled twice, although some premium tequilas may go through additional distillations for a "smoother" flavor. After distillation, tequila is either bottled right away or aged in oak barrels to enhance its distinctive character and flavor. Blanco (or silver) tequila skips the aging process and is bottled immediately after distillation. Reposado tequila is aged for two to 12 months, while añejo tequila matures for one to three years. There are also subcategories like joven, which is a blend of blanco and reposado, and extra añejo, which requires a minimum aging period of three years.

The piña is often processed in the field by hand.

The agave fields in Jalisco are beautiful and bountiful.

Trust the Label

When choosing a quality tequila for your home bar, make sure the label says 100 percent agave to ensure you're getting just that. If it doesn't, you're drinking a mixto tequila, which is only required to be 51 percent agave sugar. The rest can be other sugars, additives and flavoring—and these are typically the tequilas that lead to chants like "One tequila, two tequila, three tequila, floor."

DID YOU KNOW?

Tequila is part of the mezcal family, but unlike mezcal, it can only be made from one species of agave: the blue weber.

What goes better than tequila and lime juice? Tequila and fresh lime juice.

All great tropical drinks start with quality rum. Don't be afraid to explore the wide world of flavor profiles rum has to offer.

RUM

This is as versatile and diverse a spirit you'll find. Rum holds a captivating place in the public perception as a drink that conjures images of tropical paradises and exotic cocktails garnished with colorful umbrellas. It carries an aura of laid-back Caribbean vibes, celebration and a sense of escape.

MADE FROM: Sugarcane, either molasses (a byproduct of sugar refinement) or freshly pressed sugarcane juice

PRODUCED IN: Countries all over the world, particularly in the Caribbean, including Barbados, Guadeloupe, Guyana, Jamaica, Martinique, Trinidad, Puerto Rico, Cuba, Brazil, Venezuela

HOW TO ENJOY IT: Neat, on the rocks or in a number of classic tropical drinks like a daiquiri, piña colada or mojito. In the case of Brazil's cachaça, use it in that country's national drink: the caipirinha.

HOW IT'S MADE: Molasses or sugarcane juice is fermented and distilled to create the alcohol. The resulting liquid can be bottled immediately or aged in oak barrels for a specified period of time to create more depth and flavor as it extracts the oaky vanilla tannins from the wood. Aging requirements vary depending on where the rum is produced—some producers age it for one year, others a minimum of three years or much, much longer. White rum is typically thought to be a rum that has not been aged, but this isn't necessarily the case. Many producers will age their rum before charcoal filtering the liquid to remove the color. Because a deep brown or amber color typically means a spirit has been aged, it can be confusing seeing a clear spirit that's spent a year or more inside of a barrel. White rum is simply a blanket term to describe a rum without color. On the other hand, gold rum, dark rum or black rum usually gains its color from the wood during the aging process, but can also have color added after the fact.

Rum Around the World

Molasses-based rum tends to be sweeter, boasting flavors of caramel, toffee, vanilla and chocolate. On the other hand, rum made from fresh sugarcane juice, most known as rhum agricole (agricultural-style rum) in the French Caribbean islands of Martinique and Guadeloupe, has a grassy, earthy and vegetal taste. Cachaça, another fresh sugarcane-based rum, is produced exclusively in Brazil.

DID YOU KNOW?

Unfortunately, there is no regulation stating a rum producer can't add coloring to their product, and many do just that.

A look inside the barrel aging room for Rhum Clement, a prominent brand of rhum agricole based in Martinique.

VODKA

Despite being one of the most popular spirits worldwide, vodka is somewhat polarizing. Some criticize it as bland and flavorless—a base spirit that does nothing as a foundation. On the other hand, vodka is widely enjoyed and one of the top-selling and most consumed spirits in the world. Personally, I enjoy vodka for its subtle nuances and versatility. It's a blank canvas that invites you to get creative behind the bar.

MADE FROM: Grains like rye, wheat or even potatoes

PRODUCED IN: Countries all over the world, but particularly the U.S., Finland, Poland, Russia, Sweden and France

HOW TO ENJOY IT: Neat, on the rocks (depending on the quality of the spirit) or in some of the most popular cocktails such as the martini, cosmopolitan, greyhound, espresso martini and French 75

HOW IT'S MADE: The grains (usually rye or wheat) are mashed and fermented with yeast to convert the sugars into alcohol. It is then distilled, typically multiple times over, and sometimes filtered to remove any remaining impurities, which contributes to its clean and crisp character. Generally speaking, vodka skips the aging process and is bottled immediately after distillation.

Just Add Flavor

Vodka is one of the best spirits to infuse with different ingredients like fruit, herbs or spices to create unique cocktails and sipping experiences.

DID YOU KNOW?

Vodka was once used as a cure-all for common ailments and a disinfectant. Now we use it for martinis—another type of cure-all, in my opinion.

Pro tip: Vodka martinis can be made in a large batch, bottled, and stored in the freezer for easy pouring come time for happy hour at home with friends.

Liqueurs come in all shapes, sizes, and flavor profiles. If you can think of the flavor, there's probably a liqueur out there for it.

LIQUEURS

Let's pretend cocktails were a plate of food—if spirits are the main course, then liqueurs would be the side dish—assuming you like your sides on the sweet side. They can also be enjoyed on their own. Most liqueurs are lower in alcohol content and easier to sip than full-proof spirits, although some liqueurs can be just as boozy (e.g., Cointreau, Chartreuse or Grand Marnier).

MADE FROM: Distilled spirits that have been sweetened or flavored

PRODUCED IN: Countries all over the world

HOW TO ENJOY THEM: Neat, on the rocks or mixed in cocktails to add different flavor complexities to the drink

HOW THEY'RE MADE: Because liqueur is a very loose category, production is not standardized. Most liqueurs come with proprietary recipes and production processes that make it difficult to say how each and every liqueur is made. However, a liqueur often starts with a base spirit like brandy, rum, vodka or even tequila. Various ingredients, oils, flavors and sweetening agents are incorporated using different methods like maceration, infusion, steeping, percolation and redistillation. Liqueurs range in alcohol content from 10 to 55 percent.

A Sea of Liqueur

Since there's practically a liqueur for every type of flavor you can think of, there's no way to cover every single one in this book. However, there are several types of liqueurs found in many recipes that are helpful to know about and keep handy, so rest assured I'll provide my own recommendations throughout.

DID YOU KNOW?

Liqueurs are also called modifiers for their ability to influence the taste and flavor of a drink.

FORTIFIED WINE

Favored for their lower alcohol content (at least compared to most base spirits), fortified wines are often considered aperitifs, meaning they are enjoyed before a meal to stimulate the palate. An aperitif makes for a great welcome cocktail, prepping one's palate for an array of flavors to come. Common varieties include sherries like oloroso or Amontillado, port wine, as well as sweet and dry vermouth.

MADE FROM: Wine and a distilled spirit, typically brandy made from grapes

PRODUCED IN: Countries around the world, but predominantly France, Italy, Spain and Portugal

HOW TO ENJOY THEM: On ice or paired with fizzy beverages such as soda water, tonic water or sparkling wine. Sweet and dry vermouth in particular are extensively used in classic cocktails such as martinis, Negronis, Manhattans and Vieux Carrés.

HOW IT'S MADE: The fortified wine category includes sherry, port, Madeira, Marsala, vermouth and Muscat. All are made differently, but generally speaking, a distilled spirit is added to the wine during or after fermentation. This addition "fortifies" the wine by increasing the alcohol content and halts the fermentation process. What's left is a strong, sweet wine ready to be bottled, aged in barrels or rested in steel tanks to let the flavors meld. In the case of fortified wines like vermouth, the liquid is further steeped and infused with different herbs, spices and aromatic roots to create an herbaceous flavor profile before being bottled or aged for a period of time.

Keep It in the Fridge

Refrigerate your fortified wines after opening. Once you open the bottle, it will begin to oxidize and lose its flavor. Storing it in the fridge will help slow down the oxidation process and extend the life of the liquid.

DID YOU KNOW?

While they are not classified as liqueurs, fortified wines play a significant role in enhancing cocktails by imparting sweet, fruity, herbal, floral or nutty flavors.

Fortified wines like sherry, or vermouth are made to enjoy on their own, but it's also the key component in dozens of classic cocktails.

Traditionally Amari are served neat at room temperature, but serving it chilled or on ice with an orange slice or twist is great too.

AMARO

Amaro is a foundational drink in Italian culture and has grown into something enjoyed all around the world. From the Italian word for bitter, amaro is a bittersweet herbal liqueur. Traditionally, it was made for medicinal purposes, and it's typically enjoyed as a digestif, intended to aid digestion after a big meal. (This may be a placebo since there is no evidence to actually support this claim— still delicious though!)

MADE FROM: Infusing a base spirit with a proprietary mix of herbs, roots and spices, as well as a sweetener

PRODUCED IN: Most widely produced in Italy, though amaro can be produced anywhere in the world

ENJOY IT NEAT, mixed on ice with soda water for a fizzy lower-alcohol drink or mixed in cocktails

HOW IT'S MADE: By infusing an alcoholic base, such as a neutral spirit, grape brandy or wine, with botanical ingredients that include herbs, citrus peels, roots, spices and flowers. Amari can be light, medium-bodied or heavy with a lot of viscosity. The specific recipe, mix of ingredients and production process is usually kept top secret by the producer, which makes it difficult to say exactly how any one amaro is made. That being said, the result can be herbaceous, botanical, floral, nutty, fruity, sweet or bitter.

Low Stakes

Because amari typically come in at a lower alcohol content than most spirits, having a range available for guests is a great way to offer sippers that are both easy to prep and easy to enjoy.

DID YOU KNOW?

Some producers use as many as 130+ botanicals in their recipes. The specific blend of ingredients is often the foundation of the product and what makes each so unique, so good luck trying to find the specific recipe for any particular amaro.

Equal parts Montenegro and mezcal on ice makes for an unbelievable sipper.

Nonino is an amazing introductory amaro for any one curious to learn more.

In a Manhattan, swap out sweet vermouth with Averna amaro to make a black Manhattan.

BITTERS

Most commonly referred to as the "salt and pepper" of the cocktail world, bitters are like seasoning for your drink. Just a dash or so will heighten a drink's flavors while balancing things out.

MADE FROM: Overproof spirits steeped with herbs, spices, citrus peels and other botanical ingredients (but they can also be made from glycerin rather than a distilled spirit, creating a non-alcoholic alternative)

PRODUCED IN: Countries all over the world, but the most famous and recognizable bottle of bitters all over the world is Angostura, made by a company based in Trinidad and Tobago

ENJOY THEM SPARINGLY by adding a few dashes or drops to cocktails. Typically, bitters are not sipped on their own.

HOW IT'S MADE: Bitters are made by infusing and macerating aromatic roots, spices and other botanicals in high-proof liquor for a designated period of time.

DID YOU KNOW?

There's a popular cocktail called a Trinidad sour that calls for 1½ oz Angostura aromatic bitters, rye whiskey, fresh lemon juice and orgeat.

Start With the Classics

Since there are so many bitters on the market to choose from, I recommend starting with Angostura aromatic bitters, orange bitters and Peychaud's bitters, which are the most frequently used. Once you have the basic essentials, add on other flavors like chocolate bitters or black walnut bitters to impart seasonal or less common flavors.

Bitters add complex flavor to your cocktails while adding a bit of aesthetic flair to your home bar.

Some bartenders use bitters to create a little bit of art as a means of adding flavor and flair to a drink.

High quality mixers can elevate your overall cocktail experience.

Stocking Your Home Bar

Now that you can navigate the aisles of your local liquor store with relative ease, let's get back to the question of how to stock your home bar. Of course, I'd like you to stock your home bar with everything you need to make the drinks in this book. This book isn't about me though. It's about you—and the answer to what you should stock on your bar starts by asking a few more questions: Namely, how much space and budget do you have to work with? Fortunately, these tips will set you up for success no matter your constraints.

Consider your taste preferences. What do you enjoy drinking? Ask yourself this question and build off of your answers.

If gin and tonics are your thing, you'll naturally want to stock your home bar with a few types of gin and a variety of tonic water. Keep some fresh citrus on hand as well so you're ready to mix up your favorite G&T for your friends come Friday happy hour. If you always find yourself ordering margaritas and palomas when you're out, stock your home bar with a range of agave spirits, orange liqueur, agave, fresh limes and grapefruit soda to elevate your Taco Tuesdays.

If sipping aged spirits is your jam, your home bar should feature the likes of bourbon, cognac, rum or Scotch whisky. Consider pouring a tasting flight for you and your friends to experience the nuanced flavor notes of each one.

Once you've sorted out your preferences, your space and budget will more likely than not be the parameters that keep things from getting out of hand. Take it from my own experience: Bottles accumulate quickly, especially in a smaller apartment, so be thoughtful and deliberate about what you bring home.

I recommend starting with a few spirits you know you enjoy, then pick one or two liqueurs and the essential bitters. If you're ballin' on a budget, don't feel like you need to buy everything all at once. It's OK to develop your home bar at your own pace.

Like anything else, a number of factors influence the price of a bottle of booze, including its production process, quality, exclusivity and branding and marketing. Regardless of budget, I recommend purchasing spirits priced between $20 to $50 to start off with. Generally speaking, this should be the sweet spot when it comes to finding quality spirits to make your cocktails shine.

On the other hand, if you have the budget, plan to entertain at home or are looking to have an entire basement dedicated to your home bar, then I welcome you to indulge my ego and buy one bottle of every spirit, liqueur, fortified wine and bitters needed to make all of the drinks in this book.

To help, here is a list of what you'll need along with some brand recommendations for each. It's important to note that the world of spirits is made up of massive global brands, as well as quality national and local craft brands that deserve just as much love and respect. The following recommendations are bottles I like, for a variety of reasons. You may find a few favorites of your own. Use these recommendations as a guide, and have fun exploring. Feel free to try something new or pick one you know nothing about. Have fun with it. Alternatively, don't be so quick to definitively say what you like or don't like before you've tasted something, sat with it and played around with its applications. As you may recall, I used to hate negronis.

SPIRITS

WHISKEY
Bourbon
Old Forester, Four Roses, Buffalo Trace, Elijah Craig, Old Grandad, 1792, Woodford Reserve, Maker's Mark, Angel's Envy

Irish whiskey
Jameson, Tullamore DEW, Bushmills, Teeling

Scotch whisky
Monkey Shoulder, The Glenlivet 12, Dewar's 12, Naked Grouse, Talisker 10, Glenfiddich 12, Naked Malt Blended, Laphroaig Select, Johnnie Walker Black Label, The Famous Grouse

Rye whiskey
Rittenhouse, Sazerac, Old Overholt, Knob Creek, Wild Turkey 101, FEW Spirits Rye, High West Double Rye, Uncle Nearest Rye, Angel's Envy

BRANDY (apple brandy and cognac)
Remy Martin, Martell, Hine, Hennessy, Laird's, Berneroy Calvados, Pierre Ferrand, Courvoisier

GIN
Hendrick's, Tanqueray, Bombay Sapphire, Monkey 47, Plymouth, Ford's, Sipsmith, St. George Spirits, Empress 1908

MEZCAL
Del Maguey Vida, Montelobos, Ilegal, Madre

TEQUILA (blanco, reposado and añejo)
Espolón, Altos, Patron, Don Julio, Milagro, El Tesoro, Herradura, Gran Centenario

RUM (Aged rum and light/ unaged rum)
Appleton Estate, Flor de Caña, Don Q, The Real McCoy, Plantation, Zacapa, Bacardi, Diplomatico, Mount Gay, Rhum Clement, Brugal Añejo

VODKA
Grey Goose, Belvedere, Ketel One, Absolut, Haku, Chopin, Reyka

RED WINE (pinot noir, cabernet sauvignon or tempranillo)

WHITE WINE (sauvignon blanc, pinot grigio, chardonnay)

SPARKLING WINE (prosecco or brut champagne)

BEER (ale, light lager or wheat)

NON-ALCOHOLIC SPIRITS
(like Seedlip or Ritual Zero Proof)

LIQUEURS AND FORTIFIED WINES

ORANGE LIQUEUR
Grand Marnier, Cointreau

CAMPARI

APEROL

SWEET (RED) VERMOUTH
Carpano Antica Formula,
Dolin, Martini & Rossi,
Cinzano

DRY VERMOUTH
Dolin, Martini & Rossi,
Cinzano

AMARO MONTENEGRO

ANCHO REYES CHILE LIQUEUR

ST-GERMAIN ELDERFLOWER LIQUEUR

YELLOW CHARTREUSE

ST. GEORGE SPICED PEAR LIQUEUR

FRESH CITRUS, HERBS, FRUITS AND VEGETABLES

There are also non-boozy home bar essentials. It's nearly impossible to make the drinks in this book without having fresh citrus on hand. Citrus can be used for juice, homemade syrups or garnishing.

CITRUS
Lemons
Limes
Oranges
Grapefruit

HERBS
Mint
Rosemary
Sage
Basil
Thyme
Cilantro

NOTE: For fresh fruits and vegetables, it's best to stick with seasonal offerings and your inspiration for making cocktails with those specific ingredients.

MIXERS

Great for simple two-ingredients drinks or adding a refreshing bubbly topper to cocktails.

TONIC WATER

SODA WATER

GINGER BEER

SPARKLING WINE

GRAPEFRUIT SODA

COLA

BITTERS

ANGOSTURA AROMATIC BITTERS

ORANGE BITTERS

PEYCHAUD'S BITTERS

CHOCOLATE BITTERS

BLACK WALNUT BITTERS

What Glassware Do I Need?

You can drink out of just about anything, but the appropriate vessel can elevate your guests' experience.

Look, I have more glassware than any one person should, and I've been lugging it around from one home to another for years. I speak from experience when I say you do not need multiple sets of every type of glassware that exists… unless you, too, have an obsession with cool glassware.

Taking into account limited space, the most essential glassware to have on hand is a set of each of the following:

- Rocks glasses
- Collins glasses
- Coupe glasses
- Wine glasses
- Glass mugs

With these five types of glassware, you will be able to serve every single drink in this book and beyond. From here, everything else is nothing more than a nice-to-have.

COLLINS GLASS

Also known as a highball glass, this is for serving tall drinks with a larger volume. The name for the glass derives from the Tom Collins cocktail (pg. 112), which combines gin, lemon juice, simple syrup and soda water. I recommend a glass with a capacity between 10 to 14 ounces.

COUPE GLASS

Used for serving cocktails up, aka without ice. Coupe glasses come in various shapes and sizes, so choose one with a capacity between 4 to 6 ounces. (And make it pretty.)

WINE GLASS
One of the most common
types of glassware.
As to whether you have
stemmed wine glasses or not
is your personal preference,
though stemless glasses
tend to be more durable.

ROCKS GLASS
Also known as a tumbler or
old fashioned glass, a rocks
glass is timeless. Used for
cocktails and sipping spirits
neat or on the rocks, this is
arguably the most essential
glass to have on hand.
The capacity varies, but I
recommend something that
holds between 6 to 8 ounces.

TIKI MUG
These are fun, stylish and decorative mugs used for tropical drinks. Be warned: What starts as a funky collectible can soon turn into a passionate obsession.

GLASS MUG
Great for hot cocktails like a hot toddy or Irish coffee.

GLENCAIRN

An iconic design that's surprisingly only been around since 2001, this glass is designated specifically for whiskey and other aged spirits. Unlike the snifter glass, it has a smaller bowl and tapered neck. Combined with the flared rim, this glass lets the whiskey breathe while also capturing the drink's aromatic complexities.

SNIFTER

This glass is mostly used for aged spirits like brandy and whiskey. It has a large bowl for the drink to be swirled and a shorter mouth to trap aromas, an odd design combo that allows for a more prominent aromatic experience with every sip.

Lesson 1: Always choose a cube that fits in your glass.

Does Ice Matter?

As you'll see in the photographs in this book, I am quite particular about the ice I use in my cocktails. I consider myself an ice enthusiast, with good reason.

Ice is by far the most criminally overlooked ingredient of a good cocktail. Ice affects both the rate of dilution and the overall presentation of the drink. It can impart funky freezer flavors if you aren't careful. It's the unsung anchor of a mixed libation, hidden in a shaker or lurking below the surface of your cocktail, so treat it with the respect it deserves. In short: Heck yes, it matters.

Imagine you've just popped into a reputable cocktail bar and paid $22 for an old fashioned. You would expect to see a nice, large, clear ice cube in the glass. Now imagine if they served it to you with small, cloudy freezer ice. I'm not suggesting you lead a revolt, but for that kind of money, I can't imagine you'd want to go back. Using high-quality, well-formed ice enhances the overall experience of your drink.

STANDARD ICE CUBES

These are the most common type of ice. You can find them bagged in grocery stores or use an ice mold to make them at home. These ice cubes are approximately 1 inch by 1 inch, so they'll fit easily into various cocktail glasses. Their decent size and thickness help slow down the melting process, ensuring your drink stays chilled without losing its original flavor. These are

Cubed ice: the standard for stirred
or shaken drinks. A solid option anytime.

Large cube: adds a nice visual appeal to cocktails
and melts at a slower pace than smaller cubes.

Ice sphere: even more upscale and great for
sipping spirits on their own or stirred cocktails.

Pebble ice: most commonly used for tropical
drinks or boozier bevs that need more dilution.

perfect for cocktails that need to be shaken or stirred.

LARGE ICE CUBES

These are typically 2 inches by 2 inches and melt slower than standard ice cubes, which reduces the dilution in a cocktail. I love using a large ice cube for drinks like a Negroni or old fashioned or for simply for enjoying aged spirits as it'll keep the drink cool for a while without compromising flavor. (That said, even these melt eventually, so don't let your drink linger too long.)

SPHERES AND SPEARS

Certain ice molds can produce spheres or long cylindrical spears. Similar to large square cubes, spherical ice is great for enjoying aged spirits like bourbon or Scotch whisky and stirred cocktails because they tend

to melt at a slower pace due to a larger surface area. Cylinder-style ice is used in drinks served in a highball or Collins glass (because it fits easily into the glass) like a whiskey highball, gin and tonic or Tom Collins.

CRUSHED OR PEBBLE ICE

You can make crushed and pebble ice by smashing regular cubed ice with a mallet or blunt object. You might recognize it as the kind you get at Sonic drive-through, and it adds a nice, cold texture to cocktails. Despite its lack of a large surface area, it does tend to melt slower than plain old freezer ice, making it perfect for boozier drinks like a mint julep or drinks containing big flavors and a lot of ingredients like tiki cocktails, which can stand the additional dilution.

Carving ice at home is an almost zen experience for me, and it's an easy way to level up your home bar when entertaining. You can source large format ice from a number of sources online, or freeze a pot full of water and carve it up as needed.

A Note on Clear Ice

Large ice cubes can be clear or cloudy depending on the ice mold you use at home. To produce clear ice at home, use a mold built for directional freezing. This is a process where a liquid is frozen from the top down. Imagine a frozen lake during winter. When the air turns cold, the surface of the lake begins to freeze over. As temperatures drop, the frozen layer spreads deeper into the lake. The freezing starts from one direction and progresses uniformly, allowing impurities, air bubbles and unwanted particles to be pushed down. You can boil water or use filtered water, but if you're not using a mold that directionally freezes your ice, then it simply will not yield clear ice. As complicated as this process might sound, using clear ice in cocktails is very common, and it's never been easier to source an ice mold that produces clear ice and fits in a small freezer.

Should I Buy Syrups or Make My Own?

When it comes to the question of whether you should make or buy your syrups, the answer is both. Basic syrups like simple syrup, demerara syrup or honey syrup are incredibly easy to make at home, so you're better off doing that. You can also get creative and make seasonally inspired syrups using various ingredients like fruits, spices, tea, champagne, red wine and more. The options are endless.

As for other syrups and sweeteners like maple syrup or agave nectar, both of which I frequently use in cocktails, these are best purchased (unless you live in Vermont, have a forest on your property and possess the patience to collect, process, and store tree sap). Orgeat, an almond syrup used in tiki cocktails, requires more effort to make at home than simple syrup. In such cases, opt for high-quality brands that specialize in producing syrups for home use.

If you were to take a glimpse behind the bar of a respected cocktail establishment, you'd discover an enviable selection of essential syrups. These unique flavorings play a crucial role in creating a wide range of well-balanced drinks. Let's take a closer look at some syrups commonly found in such establishments that would be good to have at home.

Below are all the syrups you'll need for the recipes in this book. Note that when it comes to the shelf life, you want to prioritize freshness. These are not to be stockpiled like spirits. I advise making syrups based on what you're actually going to use. As a rule of thumb, if the syrup has a higher sugar content (e.g., a rich simple syrup or honey syrup) it can last up to several weeks. Fruit syrups will not last as long. That said, use your best judgment. If a syrup begins to turn cloudy or has spots or mold in it, pitch it. Recipes for my favorite syrups start on pg. 248.

Simple Syrup: Arguably the most essential syrup made by dissolving equal parts of sugar and water. It adds sweetness and balances flavors in various cocktails.

Rich Simple Syrup: A sweeter version of simple syrup, rich simple syrup adds a nice mouthfeel to drinks due to its thicker consistency. Made by combining two parts sugar to one part water.

Demerara Syrup: Similar to simple syrup, demerara syrup is made with demerara sugar, which has a rich, deep flavor profile. It lends a subtle caramel-like sweetness to drinks and accentuates the flavor notes of aged spirits like bourbon, rum or brandy (it also goes well in espresso-based cocktails). Demerara sugar is very easy to find online, but if you need to shop in person, you can substitute turbinado sugar from the supermarket.

Honey Syrup: Due to its viscosity, honey tends to harden when shaken in a cocktail with ice, so it needs to be made into a syrup if you plan to use it in your chilled drinks. To make honey syrup, combine two parts honey to one part hot water and stir to blend. This syrup imparts a unique floral sweetness to cocktails and can be a great alternative to regular simple syrup.

Grenadine: A classic cocktail syrup made from pomegranate juice and sugar, grenadine adds a sweet-tart flavor and a vibrant red hue to cocktails.

Fruit Syrups: These syrups are crafted by combining fruit juice or puree with sugar. They provide vibrant fruit flavors and can be derived from a wide range of fruits such as raspberry, strawberry, peach, pineapple and more.

Spiced Syrups: Infused with spices like cinnamon, cloves or star anise, these syrups add warmth, complexity and a touch of aromatic flair to cocktails.

Herbal Syrups: Syrups infused with tea or herbs like mint, basil or lavender offer fragrant and refreshing notes, and enhance the overall flavor profile of a drink.

MAKE YOUR OWN

1. Add 2 cups of sliced strawberries to a pot.

2. Add 2 cups of sugar to the pot.

3. Equal parts sugar to fruit will extract the juice from the strawberries on its own if left for 24 hours.

4. To speed up the process, add 1½ cups of water and bring to a light simmer on medium heat.

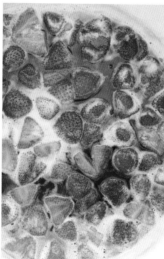

5. Once the sugar dissolves, lightly mash the strawberries and stir to combine.

6. Strain out the solids and store the syrup in a glass bottle in the refrigerator until you're ready to use!

How Should I Style My Home Bar?

Creating a great drink experience at home isn't measured in square footage, but rather in the depth of intention and thoughtfulness you put into it, both for you and your guests. Whether you live in a cozy 400-square-foot apartment in New York City, a sprawling ranch house in the heart of Texas or a charming suburban home on the outskirts of Denver, the process of crafting a delicious drink remains the same. The space you have available simply dictates how much stuff you can store. More space doesn't always mean better or more functional, so use it wisely and furnish with care.

The small apartment I lived in when I started Apartment Bartender allowed for just a bar cart. On it I stored a range of spirits, liqueurs and bitters needed to make the classic cocktails you'll find in the next section of this book. That was all the space I needed at the time, so it worked. As time passed and my collection of bottles grew, however, I wanted to show them off. I moved into a bigger apartment with a built-in shelf right next to the front door. It was a statement piece you'd see immediately upon entering, so I used to show off all my favorite aged spirits. I still had my bar cart, too, and I also set up a portion of my countertop next to the sink to operate like a bar station since I made drinks so regularly for work and entertainment. Becoming a dad meant reconfiguring my bar a third time: I ventured

A bar cabinet is a great decor piece in a smaller space and keeps bottles, glassware and barware hidden away for a cleaner aesthetic.

Ice buckets are useful for parties and gatherings, whether it be for holding ice or chilling bottles of wine or champagne. Fancy and practical.

on from the cool downtown apartment and moved my little family to the suburbs. I gradually downsized my bottle, barware and glassware collection, and hid most things away in a bar cabinet away from prying toddler hands. This is all to say: Only you know what works best for the space you have, so keep an open mind as you go. My home bar setup took on a new look in each space, but the intention and appreciation for crafting a great drink remained the same.

Your home bar is a reflection of you, your personal style, the space you have to work with and the experience you want to create. It's not one-size-fits-all and doesn't have to look any specific way.

You can have a small bar cart tucked away in a little nook with some bottles, barware and glassware on display. You can have an entire wall dedicated to your home bar and have it serve as the statement piece people see when they enter your living room.

SPIRITS, LIQUEURS AND BITTERS

Bottles occupy a significant portion of your bar setup—they're what the booze comes in, after all, so you've got to embrace them to some degree. Due to their unique shapes, colors and sizes, they can make for captivating displays as your collection grows. Bottles not only reflect your personal taste preferences—they also contribute to the atmosphere you create in your home. Their presence adds a touch of style and sophistication, making your home bar a visually appealing sight.

BARWARE AND COASTERS

Depending on the set you choose, barware and coasters can elevate the look and feel of a space. Or they can be downright tacky. Barware can be gold, copper, black or silver. I lean towards a gold or copper finish, which looks very stylish next to an etched mixing glass on a bar cart. I like my barware out and on display, both for style and accessibility should I need to mix up some drinks.

GLASSWARE

A nice set of glassware takes up quality space, and— depending on the aesthetic—can really stand out on display. You can have modern, crystal or antique glassware. Personally, I have an affinity for both minimal, simple glassware and gaudy, etched glassware that catches the sunlight peeking through the window just right. I have friends who obsess over antique stuff and find all their glassware at thrift stores. The type of glassware you buy is up to you! Don't worry if you can't fit all your glassware in your bar area. Just display the glassware you like the best or that you find yourself using the most.

CANDLES

A simple, elegant candle creates a nice atmosphere. Even something as small and innocuous as tea lights placed throughout your space will add a cozy glow and create an intimate vibe. Depending on the drinks you plan to serve, you may or may not want to use heavily scented candles, which can compete with or overwhelm a cocktail's aromatics. I typically choose mellow scents that match the season, ranging from natural wood to fresh and citrusy to earthy.

COCKTAIL BOOKS

Books make for great styling elements and conversation points. Keeping them close by to reference drink recipes comes in handy, making your bar area stylish and functional.

THE BAR BOOK

MORGENTHALER

THE FLAVOR BIBLE   KAREN PAGE AND ANDREW DORNENBURG

DAY FAUCHALD KAPLAN   COCKTAIL CODEX

KAPLAN FAUCHALD DAY   Death & Co

DECANTER

A glass decanter looks stunning in a home bar. It's also great for quick and easy pours for your guests. Pick something functional with a form you can appreciate.

DECORATIVE TOWELS

These are useful for adding texture to your bar area as well as cleaning up quick spills.

Ultimately, these styling elements are all suggestions. The arrangement and presentation of your bottles, barware, glassware and other decorative elements in your home bar setup are entirely at your discretion. Embrace the opportunity, regardless of space limitations, to curate an aesthetically pleasing environment. Take pride in the visual appeal and put thoughtful consideration into every detail. Whatever you do, do it with intention. And remember: Your home bar is still your home. It's an extension of you.

LANDON VONDERSCHMIDT

LEFT: Your bar area can be simple, straightforward and uncomplicated. Shawn, a Denver-based creative, shows off his home bar styled with bottles, bitters, artwork and a mix of plants.

RIGHT: Kelly, a photographer, turns a small area in her home into an inviting bar nook highlighting vintage glassware, quality spirits and great bottles of wine (laid horizontally to aid the aging process).

LEFT: This is a bar cart from one of my old apartments. I used it to house the liqueurs I used most frequently when making cocktails so I wouldn't have to dig them out of a cabinet while entertaining. As long as you keep a small space tidy, it can feel like a decorative element unto itself—especially with the right bottles. Just be sure to wipe them down with a warm rag after use, otherwise they'll start to get very, very sticky.

RIGHT: This bar wall in my basement is set up to feature a collection of aged spirits like whiskey, rum and brandy. It's fun to see my friends and family look through the different bottles to choose what they'll have—just like they might at a classic tavern. I also store a few sets of rocks glasses on the top shelf, so it's a simple grab, pour and sip with friends.

Just because it's a home bar, doesn't mean every bottle needs to be on display. Chris and Molly are a design and home development team based in Arizona, and their home bar area is reflective of their approach. Nearly all of their bottles are stored in the cabinets underneath so the space doesn't feel cluttered. Barware, glassware, cocktail books and art play together well to create a nice mix of decor for friends and clients.

LEFT: Bar carts can highlight your own personal style, like this desert Western theme. Justin, a fashion designer, styles his bar area with big and small cacti, an eccentric wheat wall art piece and an abundance of agave spirits. When styling your home bar area, consider elements from your personal style you'd like to reflect in your decor.

RIGHT: Take advantage of open wall space in smaller apartments. Bar carts and shelving are good storage and make otherwise empty walls fun to look at.

Your bottle collection can be simple or it can be an elaborate conversation starter. Alex, former bar manager of renowned cocktail bar Death & Co in Denver, CO, shows off a very impressive collection of bottles right in the heart of her living room.

Both Alex and her partner have careers centered in the hospitality industry, so every bottle on the shelf is unique and comes with a personal story.

How Do I Make a Drink?

So you have the tools and your home bar is stocked. Now comes the fun part. I enjoy the process of building a drink even more than imbibing. There's nothing like that first sip of a great cocktail that you took the time to make. It's the entire process for me: Measuring out the liquid ingredients, the ice rattling around in the cocktail shaker, the bar spoon gliding against the inside of the mixing glass, straining the drink over a large clear ice cube and garnishing to add a little panache. Making a drink takes time, but it's a fun process when you understand the steps involved.

As elementary as it sounds, prepping your ingredients is the first step. Just as a chef or home cook preps their ingredients and keeps everything they need in close proximity, so should you. Organize a tiny station where you can have your bottles, barware and fresh ingredients ready to get mixing. This can be directly on your bar cart, on your countertop or anywhere you feel comfortable.

The next step is to build the drink. You can do this in a cocktail shaker, in a mixing glass or directly into the glass you'll be drinking from. With the exception of hot cocktails, the goal is to properly chill and dilute your drink. Whether you shake or stir a drink, you want it to be as cold as possible while also diluting a bit using ice to balance out the ingredients. For example, if you made a martini but didn't stir the cocktail with ice first to properly chill and dilute it what you're left with is a very boozy, lukewarm martini. No bueno.

WHEN TO STIR A COCKTAIL

If a drink contains juice, dairy or egg whites, shake it (pg. 91). If it doesn't, then stir. It's that simple. If you're creating a cocktail consisting primarily of spirits, liqueur, bitters and/or syrup, then you build the drink in a mixing glass to stir. Cocktails like the old fashioned, martini, Negroni or Manhattan are all stirred drinks for this reason.

To properly stir a cocktail, first add your ingredients in a mixing glass, then fill the

CRAFTING AN OLD FASHIONED

1. Using a jigger, measure and pour ¼ oz rich simple syrup into a mixing glass.

2. Add 2 to 3 dashes aromatic bitters. (Optional: Add 2 dashes orange bitters.)

3. Next, add the spirit: Measure and pour 2 oz bourbon or rye whiskey.

4. Add ice. Using a bar spoon, stir for a few seconds to chill.

5. Using tongs, prep your rocks glass by adding one large ice cube.

6. Strain the drink into the prepared rocks glass as shown. Add a twist and enjoy.

THE ART OF THE TWIST

1. Using a peeler, carefully peel a section of orange (or lemon) as shown.

2. Examine the peel—you'll want to be sure you didn't take too much of the pith off.

3. Keep things aesthetically pleasing by trimming off the rough edges of the peel.

4. Holding both ends, gently twist the peel in opposite directions as shown.

5. Express the oil from the peel over the drink in question, then add the twist as a garnish.

6. Cheers!

glass with quality ice to chill the cocktail. Hold the bar spoon firmly by the handle and place it in the mixing glass, touching the inside edge. Stir using a smooth and gentle motion. Aim to keep the back of the bar spoon in contact with the glass as you stir to avoid aggressively sloshing the ice around, causing the drink to dilute more.

I usually stir for 10 to 15 seconds until the drink is nice and cold, slightly diluted and ready to sip. The only exception might be stirring a martini, since it typically contains more alcohol content than most spirit-forward cocktails. In this case, stirring a few seconds longer is common.

WHEN TO SHAKE A COCKTAIL

As a general rule of thumb, if a drink contains citrus juice, egg white or cream, you shake it. Drinks like a margarita, daiquiri or whiskey sour with egg white are all classic examples. There are two ways to shake a cocktail. Shaking the drink with ice is known as a "wet shake." You'll use this method for most drinks. Shaking the drink before ice is added is known as a dry "shake." The only time you do this is when you're making a cocktail that contains egg white to ensure the egg combines with the other ingredients. After you dry shake, you'll add ice to the cocktail shaker and shake again to chill the drink.

When you're shaking a cocktail, shake like you mean it. There's no need to get violent, but don't be gentle, either. I usually shake for anywhere between 12 to 15 seconds to chill and dilute the drink. You might hear elsewhere that you need to shake for 30 to 60 seconds, but that's far too long in my opinion, especially if it's a drink you're going to serve over ice anyway. The longer you shake, the more watered down your cocktail becomes, so I usually stop once the cocktail shaker gets nice and frosty on the outside. The only exception is if you're making a Ramos gin fizz, a classic cocktail that basically requires a full arm workout and 10+ minutes of shaking. (Do not order this drink during last call). Any drinks that contain egg white, like a whiskey sour, require more shaking when you take into account the need to dry shake the ingredients before adding ice for another shake.

STRAINING

After you build, chill and dilute, it's time to strain the mixture into a glass. This step prevents unwanted solids from muddying your drink.

For a shaken cocktail, you'll either use a Hawthorne strainer or the one built directly into the cobbler shaker.

Depending on the drink, you might do a "double strain," where you strain the drink directly into your fine mesh strainer over the cocktail glass to catch any unwanted solids (muddled pieces of fruit, pulp or herbs) from falling in.

For a stirred cocktail, you'll either use a Hawthorne strainer or julep strainer. You will never need to double strain a stirred cocktail.

WHEN TO BUILD A COCKTAIL IN A GLASS

If a drink contains very few ingredients (e.g., spirit and mixer), combine the ingredients directly into the glass you'll be serving in. Think about simple sippers like whiskey and soda, gin and tonic, vodka and ginger beer, orange juice and champagne. You don't need a cocktail shaker or mixing glass to make these types of libations. Also, spirit-forward drinks like a mint julep or tiki cocktails served with crushed or pebble ice are made directly in the glass and lightly agitated with a bar spoon to blend and chill the ingredients.

All About Garnishes

A drink is never done until it's garnished. An unadorned cocktail is like a gift without a bow—don't don't be a Grinch.

A garnish does so much for the overall experience of a drink: It enhances the aroma, accentuating ingredients and elevating presentation. Garnishes can be simple, such as an orange peel in an old fashioned. These garnishes add a touch of class and a bit of flavor. But they can also be over the top, like a dash of cinnamon on a flaming lime bowl that sends bursts of fire streaming into the air. These tend to be transportive and make you feel as if you're on a tropical vacation. What you garnish a drink with is only limited by your imagination. Whatever you do, though, be sure the garnish complements and/ or highlights the ingredients. Margaritas are made with lime, so they call for a lime garnish. Peach whiskey sours are made with peach and lemon, so garnish with a slice of peach and a lemon wedge. In fact, a garnish doesn't even have to be edible. I've garnished a paper plane with, well, a paper plane!

The most common garnishes I use are:

Citrus
Fruit
Herbs
Spices

CITRUS WHEELS, HALF-MOONS AND WEDGES

Pieces of citrus are tried and true garnishes, and as such are what you'll be using for a number of drinks. When cut into wheels, they add a nice, simple touch to a cocktail. Half moons are great for when entire wheels don't fit the glass, or for a cleaner look. Wedges are best when you want the option of squeezing a bit more citrus into the cocktail, like a margarita or Bloody Mary.

CITRUS PEELS

Before adding a peel to a cocktail, always express the essential oils by squeezing the back of the peel over the top of the drink. This adds a citrus-forward aroma and makes for a better sipping experience. A citrus peel can be as simple or elaborate a garnish as you want. The most common shapes are circular coins, rectangular peels or twists. Coins are good for quick and easy garnishes when you're making drinks for a large group, or if you find yourself in a bit of a rush. Rectangular peels are standard, just be sure to manicure the top, bottom and sides of the peel for a cleaner look—peels tend to look jagged and unkempt when freshly pared from the fruit. Twists start out as rectangular peels, just twisted in opposite directions at both ends. Twists are my favorite, as you'll see throughout this book.

FRUIT WEDGES, SLICES AND PIECES

If your drink includes a fruit ingredient, consider garnishing with a slice or piece of that fruit. For example, if your drink contains strawberries, garnish with a strawberry slice. If it contains pineapple, garnish with a pineapple wedge or fronds. Other fruit garnishes include speared berries, watermelon chunks, mango slices, cucumber ribbon and more. The choice is yours, so get creative!

HERBS

When it comes to herbs, you'll either garnish with a leaf, sprig or bouquet. The only time I use a bouquet is when I'm garnishing with mint. Garnishes including just one mint sprig look lonely and incomplete. Herbs like thyme or rosemary carry strong aromas and stand straight up, so individual sprigs look great in a drink. An individual leaf can make a drink feel elegant, so if that's what you're going for, consider placing the leaf on top of the drink.

Lighting one end of a sprig of rosemary smells lovely and makes for a photo-worthy cocktail.

A bouquet of mint adds a refreshing aroma, flavor and a pop of color to iced drinks.

SPICES

If your drink contains spices like star anise or cinnamon, consider using those spices as a garnish. A cinnamon stick, especially when lightly torched, adds a great visual and beautiful aroma to the drink.

If you'd rather not top your drink with a garnish, light a cinnamon stick and cover with the glass to capture the aroma.

OTHER GARNISHES

Most classic drinks come with prescribed garnishes (i.e., margaritas have lime wedges, whiskey sours have lemon wheels). Other drinks like tiki cocktails, and Bloody Marys have endless possibilities. One tiki cocktail can include pineapple fronds, citrus wheels, tiny umbrellas, brandied cherries and a lime bowl that you light on fire. A Bloody Mary can include a lemon wedge, celery stalk, piece of bacon, speared olives and a cheeseburger on top. Garnishes are meant to be fun and to enhance the experience of the drink. My only rule is to consider the drink's ingredients and choose something that you feel complements them. The rest is up to your creativity.

If you've got the time and patience, get fancy: Use a pipette to top off a drink by dotting the surface with bitters, then drag a skewer through the dots as shown.

Tiki drinks are anything but understated. Lean into the kitsch by pouring an overproof spirit into a lime bowl and igniting it followed by sprinkling cinnamon on top of the flame.
Note: You'll want to use a long match and stand back.

THE CLASSICS

When I first began navigating the passage from my post-collegiate vodka soda phase to the wider world of sophisticated cocktails, I didn't know where to start. As simple as it sounds, all I knew was that being able to make cool drinks was...cool. It seemed creative. Fun. Intentional. It struck me as a unique way to contribute to (or create) a moment, and that's what I wanted to do.

But where to start? I wanted to learn how to make the kind of drinks you'd see and order at a great cocktail bar, but at home. I didn't have much booze on hand, so I went to the liquor store and purchased a bunch of bottles I knew nothing about. I then (counterintuitively) researched what kind of drinks I could mix with what I had purchased instead of purchasing what I needed based on the recipes I wanted to make, in part because I didn't know what I wanted to make to begin with. The sheer number of cocktail recipes seemed endless, which was overwhelming. Again, where to start?

I decided to seek out expert advice. The suggestion I received from multiple sources was "Start with the classics." You should too.

Classic cocktails are classic for a reason. They're timeless. They're like the person who walks into a room and needs no introduction. We've all heard of these drinks and most likely sipped them at one point or another. They outlast trends, and they're as relevant and delicious today as they were the day they were created, with some dating back more than a century. They have roots in various countries, giving us a taste of different cultures and the chance to engage with another part of the world in the comfort of our own home.

There are dozens of classic cocktails out there. This section is not an exhaustive list in the least, but it is a collection of notable drinks anyone can shake or stir up, even if the most complicated mixed drink you've ever made is a vodka soda. They're simple and approachable, and because they're so

well loved, the ingredients can be sourced at damn near any liquor store. Understanding how to make these drinks, as well as what makes them great, will serve as the foundation for understanding how to make great drinks at home. It's pretty much where every bartender begins.

As you explore the recipes in this section, don't just see them as drinks you should know by heart—instead, let them serve as inspiration. Each of these cocktails represents a tried-and-true template you can iterate on, a springboard to creating your own variations and seasonal riffs.

All right, let's do drinks.

Old Fashioned

I 'm very romantic about this cocktail. This is the drink that made me fall in love with the world of spirits. Whiskey (I'm partial to bourbon), bitters and a little bit of sugar. That's it. It's a perfectly balanced drink when made well, with a great aroma coming from the citrus oil expressed over the glass. Old fashioneds are also my tried-and-true crowd-pleaser. The variations are endless, and we'll get to a few later in this book. Until then, you can never go wrong with this crowd-pleasing classic.

You'll often see bartenders muddling an orange slice, cherries and a sugar cube in their old fashioneds, even adding a splash of soda water. Unless you enjoy bubbly, watered-down old fashioneds with orange and cherry floaties, please don't do this. Please.

INGREDIENTS

- 2 oz bourbon or rye whiskey
- ¼ oz rich simple syrup (or demerara syrup)
- 2 dashes aromatic bitters
- 2 dashes orange bitters, optional

DIRECTIONS

1. Combine all ingredients in a mixing glass, add ice and stir to chill. Strain into a rocks glass over ice.
2. Express an orange peel (aka squeeze the pith) over the top of the drink and add to the glass for garnish.

GLASSWARE
Rocks glass

Manhattan

An iconic whiskey cocktail as famous as the island it was named after, this spirit-forward drink incorporates rye or bourbon whiskey and a bit of sweet vermouth. I prefer the spice of rye in this cocktail, but you should try it both ways and see what works for your palate.

Try this cocktail with **Scotch whisky** instead of rye and you've got yourself a variation called the **Rob Roy**. Alternatively, you can make what's called the **Reverse Manhattan**, a lower ABV (alcohol by volume) option, by swapping the ratios of whiskey and vermouth and adding an orange twist.

INGREDIENTS
- 2 oz rye or bourbon whiskey
- 1 oz sweet vermouth
- 2–3 dashes aromatic bitters

DIRECTIONS
1. Combine all ingredients in a mixing glass, add ice and stir to chill. Strain into a coupe glass.
2. Garnish with a brandied cherry.

GLASSWARE
Coupe glass

Manhattan Three Ways

You can also take this cocktail on the rocks if that's your pleasure, though it's better with a large format cube than several smaller ones. While you're mixing things up, try these variations:

ROB ROY

- 2 oz Scotch whisky
- 1 oz sweet vermouth
- 2 dashes aromatic bitters

REVERSE MANHATTAN

- 1 oz rye whiskey
- 2 oz sweet vermouth
- 2 dashes aromatic bitters

PERFECT MANHATTAN

- 2 oz rye whiskey
- ½ oz dry vermouth
- ½ oz sweet vermouth
- 2 dashes aromatic bitters

Negroni

Although it's arguably one of the best there is, this bittersweet cocktail can be an acquired taste. The bitter component comes courtesy of one of the most popular of all Italian amari: Campari. It's normal to be thrown off by a bitter flavor, but as your palate develops, you'll find this profile opens up a whole new world of drink possibilities. The negroni is your gateway.

If you substitute rye whiskey for gin, you have another classic cocktail: the Boulevardier (bool·var·dee·ay).

INGREDIENTS
- 1 oz gin
- 1 oz sweet vermouth
- 1 oz Campari

DIRECTIONS
1. Combine all ingredients in a mixing glass, add ice and stir to chill. Strain into a rocks glass over ice.
2. Garnish with an orange twist.

GLASSWARE
Rocks glass

Daiquiri

If you only memorize the recipe for one tropical drink, let it be the daiquiri. It's a superstar cocktail with only three ingredients: rum, lime and sugar. Your choice of rum will shine, so use a good one. I prefer aged rums in my daiquiris for a more robust, rich flavor profile. For a little added funk, use a Jamaican rum or rhum agricole. (White or unaged rums taste great, too.) Always always always use fresh lime juice for your daiquiri. No compromises, no exceptions.

INGREDIENTS
- 2 oz rum
- 1 oz fresh lime juice
- ½ oz rich simple syrup (or demerara syrup)

DIRECTIONS
1. Combine all ingredients in a cocktail shaker, add ice and shake to chill. Strain into a chilled coupe glass.
2. Garnish with a lime wheel.

GLASSWARE
Coupe or Nick and Nora glass

Margarita

I don't know a single person who doesn't love a good margarita. If you don't know what it is or have never tried one, you might just be living under a rock. This cocktail is great served up, on ice or even frozen. Blanco, reposado or añejo tequila all make for great margs, so it's really your call. Just make sure the tequila bottle reads "Made from 100% blue agave." Otherwise, you could be drinking blue agave mixed with anything from cane sugar to additives to coloring. Like with the daiquiri, fresh lime juice makes all the difference.

You can make a less boozy, low-calorie classic variation called a Tommy's margarita by doing away with the orange liqueur. Use 2 oz tequila, 1 oz lime juice and ½ oz agave nectar.

To rim a glass with salt, rub a lime wedge around the outer rim of the glass, and dip the rim of the glass into the salt to allow it to stick to the sides.

INGREDIENTS
- 2 oz tequila
- ¾ oz orange liqueur
- 1 oz fresh lime juice
- ¼ oz agave nectar

DIRECTIONS
1. Combine all ingredients in a cocktail shaker, add ice and shake to chill. Strain into a glass rimmed with salt, over ice. Can be a rocks glass or margarita glass.
2. Garnish with a lime wheel.

GLASSWARE
Rocks or margarita glass

Sidecar

Arguably the crème de la crème of cognac cocktails, this simple and refreshing drink contains cognac (I recommend using VSOP), orange liqueur and fresh lemon juice. I like to add just a wee bit of demerara syrup rather than having a sugar-rimmed glass, which is what the original recipe calls for. Feel free to use any brandy.

To rim a glass with sugar, rub a lemon wedge around the outer rim of the glass and dip the rim of the glass into the sugar to allow it to stick to the glass.

INGREDIENTS
- 2 oz cognac or other brandy
- ¾ oz orange liqueur
- 1 oz fresh lemon juice
- ¼ oz demerara syrup

DIRECTIONS
1. Combine all ingredients in a cocktail shaker, add ice and shake to chill. Strain into a chilled coupe glass rimmed with sugar (optional).
2. Garnish with a lemon wheel or orange twist.

GLASSWARE
Coupe or Nick and Nora glass

Tom Collins

A drink so popular they named the glass after it, the Tom Collins is a tall, bubbly, botanical gin cocktail with fresh lemon juice, simple syrup and soda water. A timeless classic with a crisp, refreshing finish perfect for any warm summer day, a Tom Collins is like lemonade's less lemony, slightly fizzy, boozy-but-not-so-boozy-you-can't-have-another cousin.

INGREDIENTS
- 2 oz gin
- 1 oz fresh lemon juice
- ¾ oz simple syrup
- 2 oz soda water

DIRECTIONS
1. In a Collins glass, combine all ingredients over ice. Lightly stir to combine.
2. Garnish with a lemon wheel or twist.

GLASSWARE
Collins glass

Moscow Mule

This vodka drink with fresh lime juice and ginger beer is crisp, refreshing and a little spicy all at once. It's typically served in a copper mug for added pizzazz, but that's more of an aesthetic thing so if you don't have a set of mule mugs don't fret—a rocks or highball glass will do. The spicy kick of ginger beer paired with the zesty, tart flavor of lime juice makes this drink an easy sipper for gatherings, parties and batching in larger amounts (think punch bowl).

Lime and ginger beer pair well with nearly every spirit, so don't feel limited to vodka. Whether you prefer gin, whiskey, rum or mezcal, any spirit of your choosing will get what you're after.

INGREDIENTS
- 2 oz vodka
- 4 oz ginger beer
- Juice from half a lime

DIRECTIONS
1. In a copper mug, add ingredients and lightly stir to combine.
2. Garnish with a lime wheel.

GLASSWARE
Copper mug

Whiskey Sour

A refreshing, citrusy cocktail that's perfect all year round, the whiskey sour traditionally includes an egg white, which creates a beautiful layer of froth on top. It also adds a silky texture and mouthfeel that makes sipping oh-so-smooth. If you're wary of using egg white, aquafaba (chickpea water) creates a similar texture and aesthetic. Or, you can skip the egg white entirely. Serve this cocktail up in a coupe glass or in a rocks glass over ice—it hits the spot either way!

Float 1 oz dry red wine after serving up the drink to make a New York Sour. The wine adds a beautiful layer on top and lends a nice dry contrast to the sweet, citrusy notes.

INGREDIENTS

- 2 oz bourbon or rye whiskey
- 1 oz fresh lemon juice
- ¾ oz simple syrup
- 1 egg white (or ¾ oz aquafaba), optional

DIRECTIONS

With egg white:

1. Combine all ingredients in a cocktail shaker and shake vigorously without ice to incorporate egg white. Add ice and shake to chill. Strain into a coupe glass and express a lemon peel over the top for aromatics.
2. Garnish with a lemon wheel and brandied cherry.

Without egg white:

1. Combine all ingredients in a cocktail shaker, add ice and shake to chill. Strain into a rocks glass with ice.
2. Garnish with a lemon wheel and brandied cherry.

GLASSWARE

Coupe glass (*with egg white*)
Rocks glass (*without egg white*)

Gimlet

A sweet, tart and refreshing gin cocktail with simple syrup and fresh squeezed lime juice, the gimlet is basically the best limeade you've ever had. This drink really lets the botanical notes of gin shine, so be sure to use a high-quality gin. It's the perfect drink for back porch or balcony sippin' on a warm day.

INGREDIENTS
- 2 oz gin
- 1 oz fresh lime juice
- ¾ oz simple syrup

DIRECTIONS
1. Combine all ingredients in a cocktail shaker, add ice and shake to chill. Strain into a coupe glass.
2. Garnish with a lime twist.

GLASSWARE
Coupe glass

Mint Julep

An herbaceous and spirit-forward cocktail, the mint julep is one of those drinks that gets better with every sip. There's not much to it, just bourbon, fresh mint and a little simple syrup, so my only advice is not to skimp on the mint: Nobody likes a wilted garnish. Each sip is like sticking your nose in a bushel of mint. The aroma and scent mint provides is a key aspect to the flavor and enjoyment of this drink. This cocktail is specifically served with pebble ice, which opens it up as it sits so it becomes even easier to drink. It has a long and rich history as the official cocktail of the Kentucky Derby, which should tell you that an ice-cold mint julep and a hot summer day go hand in hand…and don't forget your wide-brimmed hat.

The Mint Julep has been beloved for so long it's mentioned in many great novels like *The Great Gatsby* and *Gone with the Wind*.

INGREDIENTS
- 5–6 fresh mint leaves
- ½ oz simple syrup
- 2½ oz bourbon

DIRECTIONS
1. In a julep cup, add mint leaves and simple syrup. Gently muddle the mint to release the flavor and aromatics (don't crush it). Add the bourbon and top with pebble ice. Lightly stir, then add more ice.
2. Garnish with a bouquet of mint.

GLASSWARE
Julep cup or rocks glass

Jungle Bird

This tiki-style drink is simple and approachable, with fewer ingredients than most tiki cocktails. It's fruity, slightly bitter and everything that's perfect about tropical bevvies. Traditionally, blackstrap rum is used, but feel free to use any aged rum you have on hand.

INGREDIENTS

- 2 oz aged rum
- ¾ oz Campari
- 1½ oz fresh pineapple juice
- ½ oz fresh lime juice
- ½ oz simple syrup

DIRECTIONS

1. Combine all ingredients in a cocktail shaker, add ice and shake to chill. Strain into a rocks glass over crushed or pebble ice.
2. Garnish with a brandied cherry, a bouquet of mint and pineapple fronds.

GLASSWARE
Rocks glass

Whiskey Highball

This two-ingredient cocktail features whiskey and soda water. If that seems too easy, that's because it is—but that doesn't make it bad. Remember, a great drink doesn't have to be a complicated one. However, attention to detail matters. This cocktail is best served nice and cold, so be sure to freeze your highball glass and chill your soda water beforehand.

I prefer Scotch whisky to be the star of the show here, but you can use any whiskey you enjoy sipping: bourbon, rye, American single malt, Japanese whisky, Irish whiskey, etc. Have your pick, but as always, use a quality spirit.

In Japanese culture, the whisky highball is an art form. From the whisky selection to the ice to the frosty highball glass and the chilled soda water, the build of this cocktail is a ritual to be taken seriously. If you ever want a masterclass in drink perfection, dig into Japanese whisky highball culture.

INGREDIENTS
2 oz whiskey
4 oz soda water

DIRECTIONS
1. In a highball glass filled with ice, add the whiskey and chilled soda water. Lightly stir to combine.
2. Garnish with a lemon twist.

GLASSWARE
Highball glass

Gin & Tonic

Like the whiskey highball, this cocktail is very simple but packs a complex flavor profile. The secret is using quality gin and tonic water to really let the botanicals of your gin shine. Also, the garnish doesn't always have to be a lime. Consider garnishing your G&Ts with different types of citrus and herbs that will complement your gin of choice.

Gin & tonics are sacred in Spain. Spanish-style G&Ts are served in a goblet and garnished with a range of citrus and botanicals for an even more colorful and aromatic experience.

INGREDIENTS
- 2 oz gin
- 4 oz tonic water

DIRECTIONS
1. In a Collins glass filled with ice, add the gin and chilled tonic water. Lightly stir to combine.
2. Garnish with fresh citrus and herbs that pair best with the botanicals of your gin (e.g., grapefruit, lime, lemon, rosemary, thyme, mint, cucumber).

GLASSWARE
Collins glass

Paloma

I once heard this cocktail described as the taller, more refreshing sister of a margarita, and I haven't forgotten it since. Requiring just tequila, lime and grapefruit soda, this drink is a simple one to mix up for game day or game night. Add a squeeze of fresh grapefruit juice to brighten up the grapefruit soda.

Swap out the tequila for mezcal to create a refreshing and smoky mezcal paloma.

INGREDIENTS

Pinch salt, optional
2 oz tequila
Juice from half a lime
4 oz grapefruit soda

DIRECTIONS

1. Rim a Collins glass with salt. Fill the glass with ice, then add the tequila and lime juice. Top with grapefruit soda.
2. Garnish with a grapefruit wedge and lime wheel.

GLASSWARE

Collins glass

Sazerac

A drink with a rich history and hailing from New Orleans, this moody, spirit-forward cocktail is a mix of cognac (or rye whiskey), sugar, bitters and a rinse of absinthe for a hint of anise and licorice flavor. The anise flavor profile unique to this drink also comes specifically from Peychaud's bitters— without this ingredient, you don't have a Sazerac. Don't forget to chill your glassware before building this drink. After all, the devil's in the details.

INGREDIENTS
- 2 oz rye whiskey or cognac VSOP
- ¼ oz demerara syrup
- 2-3 dashes Peychaud's bitters
- 2 dashes aromatic bitters
- Absinthe

DIRECTIONS
1. Before building the drink, place a cocktail glass in the freezer to chill. In a mixing glass, combine the first four ingredients. Add ice and stir thoroughly. Rinse the chilled glass in absinthe. Strain the drink into the glass.
2. Garnish with a lemon twist.

GLASSWARE
Rocks glass

Martini

The martini is one of the most iconic cocktails around. But no one seems to agree on the best way to make it. Gin or vodka? (Gin.) Stirred or shaken? (Stirred.) Lemon twist or olives? (Trick question if you prefer a cocktail onion.) However you like your martini, it's probably different than how your aunt likes hers. Despite this, you and your aunt can both agree that crafting a great martini at home can make you feel as sophisticated as they come. Because there are so many variations, it's always good to start with the tried-and-true classic recipe before you refine your own variations.

You can make this drink a dirty martini by subbing in vodka (or stick with gin) and adding ½ oz olive brine for a more salty, savory flavor profile. Dirty martinis are typically garnished with an olive or three.

INGREDIENTS
- 2½ oz gin
- ½ oz dry vermouth
- 1–2 dashes orange bitters

DIRECTIONS
1. Before building the drink, chill a glass in the freezer.
2. In a mixing glass, combine all the ingredients. Add ice and stir thoroughly. Strain into the chilled glass.
3. Garnish with a lemon twist.

GLASSWARE
Coupe, Martini or Nick and Nora glass

French 75

The quintessential cocktail for all celebratory moments, elegant get-togethers and New Year's Eve, it's believed the original French 75 contained Cognac rather than gin, but either spirit works well. Now, let's raise a toast!

INGREDIENTS
- 1 oz gin or cognac
- ½ oz fresh lemon juice
- ½ oz simple syrup
- 3–4 oz sparkling wine (I recommend a brut or prosecco)

DIRECTIONS
1. Combine the first 3 ingredients in a cocktail shaker. Add ice and shake to chill. Strain into a champagne flute and top with chilled sparkling wine.
2. Garnish with a lemon twist.

GLASSWARE
Champagne flute

Spritz

A spritz is a bubbly summer cocktail usually made with a liqueur, soda water and sparkling wine. An Aperol spritz is among the most common (I consider it a modern classic). Aperol is an Italian amaro (definitely less bitter than Campari), but you can swap it out for any amaro or other liqueur.

I like Aperol for a classic spritz but prefer Amaro Montenegro or elderflower liqueur when entertaining.

INGREDIENTS

- 2 oz Aperol
- 1 oz soda water
- 2–3 oz sparkling wine (I recommend a brut or prosecco)

DIRECTIONS

1. Combine all ingredients in a wine glass over ice. Lightly stir to combine.
2. Garnish with an orange wedge.

GLASSWARE
Wine glass

INGREDIENTS
- 4 oz hot coffee (medium or dark roast)
- 2 oz Irish whiskey
- ½ oz demerara syrup
- 2 oz heavy whipping cream

DIRECTIONS
1. Preheat the glass mug by filling it with hot water. Brew a fresh cup of hot coffee. Discard the hot water in the mug, then add in the whiskey, syrup and top with coffee. Lightly stir to combine.
2. In a cocktail shaker, add the heavy whipping cream (sweeten with ½ oz demerara syrup if desired). Shake vigorously until it reaches a light, whipped and fluffy consistency. Using the back of a bar spoon, layer the top of the cocktail with the whipped cream.
3. Garnish with freshly grated nutmeg.

GLASSWARE
Glass mug or dessert glass

Irish Coffee

Name a better pair than coffee and whiskey...I'll wait. This hot cocktail is designed to pick you up and mellow you out at the same time. It makes for a great dessert drink, Sunday brunch sipper or holiday cocktail (especially garnished with a little fresh nutmeg). Obviously, Irish coffee calls for Irish whiskey, but feel free to use whatever whiskey you want. Either way, this drink is a love language. Create it with care and watch your guests swoon.

Espresso Martini

The only thing better than a hot cup of coffee at breakfast is an espresso martini at happy hour. This is the perfect pick-me-up cocktail. Using freshly brewed espresso is key when it comes to building bold flavor. Vodka is traditionally used, but I'm a fan of aged rum as well.

INGREDIENTS
- 2 oz vodka
- 1 oz fresh espresso
- ½ oz simple syrup

DIRECTIONS
1. Combine all ingredients in a cocktail shaker and shake with ice. Strain into a coupe glass.
2. Garnish with three coffee beans.

GLASSWARE
Coupe glass

Hot Toddy

A warm, boozy cocktail with whiskey, honey, hot water and lemon, a toddy is perfect for chilly fall days or cold winter evenings with friends. Although I would not recommend alcohol as a health remedy, you might hear that hot toddies are a go-to cocktail to help soothe a sore throat and relax the body during a mild cold.

I like a hot toddy any time, but if you're serving these as the leaves start to change, I typically include a cinnamon stick as a secondary garnish to add extra fall flavor.

INGREDIENTS
- 2 oz whiskey
- ½ oz honey
  Juice from half a lemon
- 4 oz hot water

DIRECTIONS
1. Preheat a glass mug by filling it with hot water. Discard the hot water, then add the whiskey, honey, lemon juice and top with hot water. Lightly stir to combine.
2. Garnish with a lemon wheel.

GLASSWARE
Glass mug

Mojito

A Cuban cocktail featuring rum, lime, mint, sugar and soda water, a mojito is one of those drinks I love to drink but don't always love to mix (especially for larger crowds, where the muddling of mint starts to wear on your wrists). But the combination of these ingredients makes for a sweet, tangy and refreshing drink that's perfect for summer sipping, ideally on a beach with a group of close friends.

INGREDIENTS
- ¾ oz simple syrup
- 6–7 mint leaves
- 3–4 fresh lime wedges
- 2 oz white rum
- 1–2 oz soda water

DIRECTIONS
1. Combine simple syrup, mint and lime in a Collins glass. Gently muddle the mint and lime to release the juice and flavor. Add in the rum and crushed (or pebble) ice, then lightly stir to combine. Add more ice and top with soda water.
2. Garnish with a bouquet of mint.

GLASSWARE
Collins glass

Bloody Mary

Touted as the ultimate brunch cocktail—or essential hangover cure given its spicy, hearty and savory ingredients—the Bloody Mary is a can't-miss classic that's limited only by your imagination. That said, the garnish might just be the best part. Sure, you can go with a lime wedge and an olive, but I've seen it garnished with a bacon cheeseburger slider, a whole snow crab leg and a half-dozen shrimp—it's an excuse to get a little weird. Whatever garnish you choose, make sure you nail the drink itself before you go nuts on add-ons.

Swap out the vodka for tequila and you've got yourself a Bloody Maria. Use gin, and you've got a Red Snapper.

INGREDIENTS
- 2 oz vodka
- 4 oz tomato juice
- Juice from half a lemon
- 1 Tbsp horseradish
- ½ oz Worcestershire sauce
- 2–3 dashes hot sauce (typically Tabasco)
- Pinch of salt and black pepper

DIRECTIONS
1. Combine all ingredients in a cocktail shaker, add ice and shake gently. Strain into a pint glass over ice.
2. Garnish with a celery stalk, lemon wedge and slice of crispy bacon.

GLASSWARE
Collins or pint glass

Cosmopolitan

A relatively new addition to the classic canon, the cosmo has become so ubiquitous that it can no longer be considered trendy. Vodka, orange liqueur, cranberry and freshly squeezed lime juice shaken together makes for one easy sipping cocktail. Nobody will turn down a freshly mixed cosmopolitan at a summer kickback. All the more reason to make a pitcherful.

INGREDIENTS
- 2 oz vodka
- ¾ oz orange liqueur
- ¼ oz simple syrup
- 1 oz unsweetened cranberry juice
- ½ oz lime juice

DIRECTIONS
1. Combine all ingredients in a cocktail shaker and shake with ice. Strain into a coupe glass.
2. Garnish with a lime wheel or orange twist.

GLASSWARE
Coupe glass

Sangria

This traditional Spanish libation is by far one of the best drinks to savor with friends and family. It's a versatile classic you can make with red or white wine, fresh fruit and a bit of brandy. The drink benefits from resting a bit to let the ingredients meld, so I recommend prepping several hours before your gathering or even the night before—just add the sparkling water right before you serve so the bubbles are fresh.

INGREDIENTS

- 1 bottle Spanish red wine
- 2 oz brandy
- 2 oz orange liqueur
- Juice from 1 whole orange
- 2-3 strawberries, sliced
- 1 lemon, sliced
- 1 orange, sliced
- 1 apple, sliced
- 3-4 oz sparkling water

DIRECTIONS

1. Add all ingredients except sparkling water to a pitcher and stir to combine. Refrigerate for several hours (or up to 24 hours), periodically stirring to mix. When ready to serve, top with sparkling water and serve over ice in a wine glass.
2. Garnish with an orange slice, lemon wheel or mint sprig, or combine as preferred.

GLASSWARE
Wine glass

Mai Tai

Created by a tiki culture icon nicknamed Trader Vic, this is one of the OG tiki cocktails. This tropical drink highlights rum, dry curaçao (a type of orange liqueur), fresh lime and orgeat (a sweet almond syrup) and will transport you to the beach even if you're landlocked.

INGREDIENTS
- 2 oz aged rum (commonly Jamaican rum)
- ½ oz orange liqueur (traditionally dry Curaçao)
- 1 oz fresh lime juice
- ½ oz orgeat

DIRECTIONS
1. Combine all ingredients in a cocktail shaker and shake with ice. Strain into a rocks glass over ice.
2. Garnish with a mint bouquet, brandied cherry and lime wheel.

GLASSWARE
Rocks glass

Piña Colada

An iconic tropical drink synonymous with relaxing beach vacations or getting caught in the rain. A sweet and delectable combination of rum, pineapple, fresh lime and coconut, you don't have to buy a cheap mix to make it. In fact, you shouldn't!

INGREDIENTS
- 2½ oz aged rum
- 1½ oz pineapple juice
- ½ oz fresh lime juice
- 1 oz cream of coconut

DIRECTIONS
1. Combine all ingredients in a cocktail shaker with ice and shake vigorously. Strain into a hurricane glass over crushed ice.
2. Garnish with a pineapple slice, lime wheel and brandied cherry.

GLASSWARE
Hurricane glass

Greyhound

Simplicity is a beautiful thing. In this case, all you need is vodka (or gin) and freshly squeezed grapefruit juice. This citrus-forward sipper is great for warm spring weather. I love to add just a bit of simple syrup to round out the bitter edges of the fresh grapefruit.

INGREDIENTS
- 2 oz vodka or gin
- 4 oz fresh grapefruit juice
- ½ oz simple syrup, optional

DIRECTIONS
1. Combine all ingredients over ice in a Collins glass. Lightly stir to combine.
2. Garnish with a grapefruit slice.

GLASSWARE
Collins glass

Bee's Knees

One of my favorite spring cocktails with gin, honey syrup and fresh lemon juice. This drink dates back to Prohibition when the term "bee's knees" was synonymous with "best." The floral and honey-forward notes play well with the botanicals in gin, making it one of the best sippers around.

INGREDIENTS
- 2 oz gin
- ¾ oz honey syrup
- 1 oz fresh lemon juice

DIRECTIONS
1. Combine all ingredients in a cocktail shaker and shake with ice. Strain into a rocks glass over ice.
2. Garnish with a lemon twist.

GLASSWARE
Rocks glass

Gold Rush

A refreshing and floral cocktail with bourbon, honey syrup and freshly squeezed lemon juice. With its roots in a classic whiskey sour, this variation was created by the late world-renowned bartender Sasha Petraske, who also founded the iconic cocktail lounge Milk & Honey. Though he is gone, his drink lives on, blessing us with easy sippin' and great moments with loved ones.

INGREDIENTS
- 2 oz bourbon or rye whiskey
- ¾ oz honey syrup
- 1 oz fresh lemon juice

DIRECTIONS
1. Combine all ingredients in a cocktail shaker and shake with ice. Strain into a rocks glass over ice.
2. Garnish with a lemon wheel.

GLASSWARE
Rocks glass

Milk Punch

This delicious, simple drink is best served during the holidays, a good brunch or as a dessert cocktail. The original recipe calls for simple syrup (see pg. 249) and vanilla extract, but we're simplifying things by using vanilla syrup.

INGREDIENTS
- 2 oz brandy (or bourbon)
- 2 oz whole milk
- 1 oz vanilla syrup (see pg. 249)

DIRECTIONS
1. Combine all ingredients in a cocktail shaker and shake vigorously with ice. Strain into a rocks glass; ice is optional.
2. Garnish with freshly grated nutmeg.

GLASSWARE
Rocks glass

SEASONAL & SIGNATURE RECIPES

My approach to drinks at home has always been about considering the moments that bring people together: birthdays, graduations, holidays and other celebratory events. I also like to consider the current season and what flavors are most prominent at the moment. When making drinks at home, it's normal to use common household pantry items as well as what's fresh and available at your local grocery store. As a photographer, I approach making drinks from a visual perspective. When photographing cocktails, my goal is to make them look so damn pretty that the viewer immediately thinks, "Wow, I have to try this."

I can get nerdy and intricate with the best of them, but when I'm entertaining and making drinks at home I prefer to keep things relatively uncomplicated. Still, "uncomplicated" doesn't mean "unstructured." It's not so much about throwing booze into a glass and seeing how it turns out—it's about understanding the building blocks of a good drink and playing with different flavors to create something greater than the sum of its parts.

In the beginning of my journey, a friend advised me to check out a book called *The Flavor Bible*. It's a culinary reference book by Karen Page and Andrew Dornenburg and one of the titles that expanded my view on what's possible with flavor combinations. It's quite literally an encyclopedia of flavors and their pairings. It's books like this and *The Flavor Thesaurus* by Niki Segnit that I use all the time as reference points for understanding which flavors interact best. If I found myself with a flavored liqueur I didn't know what to do with, I'd research that particular flavor to see what best complements it. I'd pick out one or two flavors and find a way to incorporate them into a drink. I'd infuse a spirit with one then make a syrup with the other, and voilà: a custom home cocktail with a range of flavors that bring out the best in each other.

Spring and summer inspire light and bright cocktails with unaged spirits like gin, vodka, light rum and blanco tequila. Fresh ingredients like berries, watermelon, pineapple, lavender, mint and citrus shine. In fall and winter, spice-forward flavors with warming notes of vanilla, cinnamon, pomegranate, apple, thyme, rosemary and chocolate stand out. Aged spirits such as bourbon, rum, brandy and reposado tequila warm the bones, a welcome gift during the chillier months of the year.

As noted in the previous section, classic cocktails are not only really good drinks but also templates for creating your own iterations. The flavor combinations you can mix and bring to life in a glass are endless, but seasonal ingredients make those choices pop. Choose wisely, but feel free to experiment (preferably before you host a party). Prioritize freshness, then build your drink on a foundation of the things that work best according to your taste.

The drinks that follow are a collection of some of the most memorable ones I've had over the years, imbibed at cocktail bars throughout my journey and tasted on worldly travels. Some are signature recipes, others are seasonal interpretations of classic drinks that I've gotten a lot of mileage out of at my own personal gatherings. With these recipes by your side, you'll find that a delicious drink can elevate just about any moment, because when it's made with precision and care, that's reason enough to celebrate.

My hope is that you view this section not only as a series of recipes but as a conduit for your creativity. These drinks are the end result of my original goal: to bring a curated cocktail experience into a small corner of my home. If you approach your own process with intention and continue to ask yourself "What would make my guests feel most at home?" the resulting drinks will astound everyone who walks through your front (or side, or back) door. As much as I'd love for you to make every drink presented, I also want you to put thought and intention into the moments you want to create for yourself and your guests.

I believe each of those moments starts with a great drink. If you agree, I think you'll find the rest will take care of itself.

Pineapple Mezcal Sour

SEASON: SPRING & SUMMER

This is one of my go-to drinks year-round (but it's especially refreshing in the warmer months), as it's simple to mix up if I'm looking to give guests a unique tasting experience. Mezcal and pineapple are a match made in heaven. The earthy and smoky notes of mezcal meld with the tropical, sweet flavor of pineapple, and the acidity of the lime marries the two together. When prepping your pineapple syrup, freeze a few of the best-looking pineapple fronds to use as a future garnish. Having this cocktail in your repertoire never disappoints. I've said it before and I'll say it again: Use fresh lime juice.

INGREDIENTS
- 2 oz mezcal
- ¾ pineapple syrup (see pg. 249)
- 1 oz lime juice

DIRECTIONS
1. Combine all ingredients in a cocktail shaker, add ice and shake to chill. Strain into a coupe glass.
2. Garnish with a lime wheel.

GLASSWARE
Coupe or Nick and Nora glass

Rosé & Co.

SEASON: SPRING & SUMMER

You know when you see a server carrying a tray of eight enticing glasses out to a table celebrating something special and you immediately want one based on looks alone? This is that drink. There's something about a bubbly red cocktail that makes heads turn. There's a lot to love: It's bright, fruity, effervescent and refreshing. Strawberries are one of the best summer ingredients for when you're craving something sweet and juicy. Add a little rosé to the mix and you've got the ultimate rose-colored accompaniment for any rooftop get-together.

INGREDIENTS
- 1½ oz vodka
- ½ oz lime juice
- ½ oz simple syrup
- 2 fresh strawberries
- Brut rosé

DIRECTIONS
1. Combine the first 4 ingredients in a cocktail shaker, then muddle the strawberries. Add ice and shake to chill. Fine strain into a coupe glass and top with chilled rosé.
2. Garnish with a strawberry slice.

GLASSWARE
Coupe or Nick and Nora glass

Aloha Friday

SEASON: SPRING & SUMMER

Early in my career, I photographed seasonal menus for Undertow, a renowned tiki bar in Phoenix founded by a dear friend and bar proprietor, Jason Asher. This was the start of my fascination with tiki drinks and the way they incorporate a range of different rums and tropical flavors to create something unique. I've always enjoyed mixing tropical-style drinks at home— they make you feel like you're on island time.

There's no need to hold out for the best workday of the week when you can shake up your own cup of weekend-worthy goodness in a flash. A tiki drink is as much about presentation as taste, so put some effort into the garnish, especially the lightly torched cinnamon stick. This adds a nice trail of smoke that's sure to have your guests seeking out the source of its captivating aroma.

Note: Take care when igniting the cinnamon stick lest your mint go up in flames. Light one end, allow it to burn for a moment or two, then blow out the flame so that it creates a lovely, fragrant trail of smoke before placing the cinnamon stick on top of the drink.

INGREDIENTS
- 2 oz aged rum
- ½ oz orange liqueur
- 1 oz grapefruit juice
- ½ oz lime juice
- ½ oz pineapple syrup (see pg. 249)
- 3–4 dashes aromatic bitters

DIRECTIONS
1. Combine all ingredients in a cocktail shaker, add ice and shake to chill. Strain into a Collins glass and top with crushed or pebble ice.
2. Garnish with a bouquet of mint and lightly torched cinnamon stick.

GLASSWARE
Collins glass

Blackberry Buck

SEASON: SPRING & SUMMER

Growing up, we had a blackberry bush in our backyard. Each year, I'd patiently wait for the fruit to ripen so I could pick each berry and immediately pop it into my mouth. Inspired by those memories of life's simple pleasures, this refreshing cocktail is perfect for backyard hangs. Blackberry and ginger create a delicious sweet and spicy combination, and the resulting color makes it a visual stunner. Whiskey is a great base, but I'm somewhat biased toward aged spirits in general, so feel free to use the alcohol of your choice—the other flavors in the cocktail truly pair well with anything.

Swap out the blackberries for any other berry (e.g., strawberries, blueberries, raspberries) or other fruity flavors of your choice.

INGREDIENTS
- 2 oz bourbon or blended Scotch whisky
- 1 oz lemon juice
- ¾ oz honey syrup
- 3–4 blackberries
- 2 oz ginger beer

DIRECTIONS
1. Combine the first 4 ingredients in a cocktail shaker, then muddle the blackberries. Add ice and shake to chill. Fine strain into a Collins glass over ice and top with ginger beer.
2. Garnish with a lemon wheel, mint leaf and speared blackberry.

GLASSWARE
Collins glass

Negroni di Aquila

SEASON: SPRING & SUMMER

This drink will forever remind me of springtime in Chicago. I was sitting on the patio at Longman & Eagle, one of my favorite spots on the northwest side of the city, and saw this drink on the menu. Aperol, sweet vermouth and prosecco sounded like the perfect match for sunny skies and 70-degree weather. Boy, was it fitting. This is basically a cross between an Aperol spritz and Negroni Sbagliato (Campari, vermouth and prosecco), making for a crisp, sweet and slightly bitter drink that quickly became one of my favorite sippers. If you're looking for springtime in a glass, this is the one.

INGREDIENTS
- 1 oz Aperol
- 1 oz sweet vermouth
- 4 oz prosecco

DIRECTIONS
1. Combine all ingredients in a wine glass over ice and lightly stir to combine.
2. Garnish with an orange wedge.

GLASSWARE
Wine glass

Frozen Mango Margarita

SEASON: SPRING & SUMMER

Growing up in the blistering heat of Arizona summers, my natural inclination in the summertime is to reach for drinks as cold as humanly possible—I'm talkin' the kind of cold that gives you brain freeze—hence my affinity for frozen margaritas. Mango is my choice because it's a summer fruit unlike any other and lends a sweet, almost silky texture to this drink. You can swap out the mango for any fruit of your choice (strawberries, blackberries or watermelon all work well) to create different variations, but mango has my whole heart.

Float ½ oz mezcal on top of the drink for a nice smoky contrast and a little extra kick.

INGREDIENTS
- 2 oz blanco tequila
- ¾ oz orange liqueur
- 1 oz lime
- ½ oz agave nectar
- 4–5 mango chunks

DIRECTIONS
1. Combine all ingredients in a blender and add 1 cup ice. Blend to a smoothie-like consistency. Pour into a margarita glass rimmed with Tajín (chili lime seasoning).
2. Garnish with a slice of mango and fresh mint.

GLASSWARE
Margarita glass

Lavender
Spring Cooler

SEASON: SPRING & SUMMER

There's nothing better after a long, cold winter than that first sunny, 70-degree day of the year that gets you excited to venture outdoors again. Spring truly is a celebration of changing seasons, and the addition of lavender makes this drink taste like life is in full bloom. The botanical flavor profile of gin is a perfect match for prominent spring flavors like lavender, grapefruit and lemon. Add some bubbles for a touch of effervescence and you've got an outdoor sipper that's perfect for any sunny celebration.

INGREDIENTS
- 2 oz gin
- 1 oz lavender syrup (see pg. 249)
- 1 oz grapefruit juice
- ½ oz fresh lemon juice
- 2 oz soda water

DIRECTIONS
1. Combine all ingredients in a Collins glass, add ice and lightly stir to combine.
2. Garnish with a sprig of lavender and grapefruit slice.

GLASSWARE
Collins glass

Sunset Boulevard

SEASON: SPRING & SUMMER

It was golden hour on a beautiful Tuesday in West Hollywood. I was making drinks for the evening at a dreamy Art Deco-style cocktail bar not far from Sunset Boulevard: Bibo Ergo Sum (Latin for "I drink, therefore I am"). As elevated as this spot felt, it was also intimate and welcoming, the kind of place where you could relax and enjoy a cocktail and a quality conversation. This is one of the drinks I put on the menu for that night and one that was ordered again and again and again. It's tropical, herbaceous and so delicious. I wanted to serve something that was simple to make yet elevated in taste so I included yellow chartreuse. It's a favorite liqueur of mine, and the distinct and complex flavor it adds makes even the most straightforward cocktails stand out. Vodka provides a blank canvas for this spiced herbal liqueur to mesh with the floral notes of honey syrup and the tangy, sweet tropical notes of lime and pineapple. It's the kind of drink that brings me back to that golden hour in LA.

If you don't have yellow chartreuse, you can swap it out for orange liqueur for sweetness or a chile liqueur like Ancho Reyes for added spice. Note: When juicing your pineapple, be sure to save a frond for the garnish.

INGREDIENTS
- 2 oz vodka
- ½ oz yellow chartreuse
- 1 oz pineapple juice
- ½ oz lime juice
- ½ oz honey syrup

DIRECTIONS
1. Combine the ingredients in a cocktail shaker, add ice and shake to chill. Strain into a coupe glass.
2. Garnish with a lime wheel and pineapple frond.

GLASSWARE
Coupe glass

Garden Party

SEASON: SPRING & SUMMER

Come summertime, I'm big on juicing fresh produce, and cucumber ranks high on that list. This refreshing green drink is the perfect choice for someone who wants to have it all—a healthy green juice and a shot of something stronger, a merging of the botanical base spirit (hello, gin) with smoky mezcal. Who says you can't stay hydrated while enjoying the strong stuff? Just remember not to knock this back like a lemongrass shot. It goes down smoothly, so enjoy it while it lasts.

To make cucumber ribbons for garnish, use a knife to trim the ends from the cucumber. Use a vegetable peeler (or Y-peeler) to carefully slice the cucumber lengthwise into a long, thin ribbon. Line the inside of the glass with the cucumber ribbon, then add ice to the glass.

INGREDIENTS
- 1 oz gin
- 1 oz mezcal
- 1 ½ oz fresh cucumber juice
- ½ oz fresh lemon juice
- ½ oz agave nectar

DIRECTIONS
1. Combine all ingredients in a cocktail shaker and shake with ice. Strain into a rocks glass over ice.
2. Garnish with a bouquet of mint and lemon slice.

GLASSWARE
Rocks glass

Passion Fruit Rum Old Fashioned

SEASON: SPRING & SUMMER

Over the years, I spent some time in the Caribbean working with Spiribam, a company known for its portfolio of fine spirits. I walked through the sugarcane fields of Martinique and tasted the fresh pressed sugarcane juice before it was made into agriculture rum. I sailed a catamaran through the Caribbean and sipped rum old fashioneds while cruising by the Pitons of Saint Lucia. A rum old fashioned will always remind me of those moments. While I've grown fond of Caribbean rums, there are so many great types of rum out there. This is a great drink to experiment with by using multiple types of rum (even combining them). For the syrup, you can always use a rich simple syrup or demerara syrup to make it a classic rum old fashioned, but passion fruit syrup makes the drink even more summery. This one will have you packing your bags for the first available flight to your favorite island.

INGREDIENTS
- 2 oz aged rum
- ¼ oz passion fruit syrup (see pg. 249)
- 2 dashes orange bitters
- 2 dashes aromatic bitters

DIRECTIONS
1. Combine all ingredients in a mixing glass, add ice and stir to chill. Strain into a rocks glass over ice.
2. Garnish with a lime twist.

GLASSWARE
Rocks glass

Spicy Cilantro Margarita

SEASON: SPRING & SUMMER

I have a big Mexican family, and if there are two ingredients that we always stock at home, they're cilantro and jalapeños. Spicy margaritas are the cocktail my family requests from me the most. A classic margarita is amazing on its own, but adding the heat of jalapeño kicks things up a notch. Cilantro is a cool-weather herb, so it's at its freshest in the spring and adds a great vegetal flavor to the spice of jalapeño.

This drink definitely has a kick to it, so depending on how many jalapeño coins you add, it could turn out too spicy. Be mindful of your guests' spice tolerance: Start out by muddling one jalapeño coin, have your guest try the drink, then add extra coins as garnish if they'd like to amp up the heat.

INGREDIENTS
- 2 oz blanco tequila
- ¾ oz orange liqueur
- 1 oz lime juice
- ¼ oz agave nectar
  Handful cilantro leaves and stems
- 2–3 jalapeño coins with seeds (more if desired)

DIRECTIONS
1. Combine all ingredients in a cocktail shaker. Muddle the cilantro and jalapeño. Add ice and shake to chill. Fine strain into a rocks glass (rimmed with salt or Tajín) over ice.
2. Garnish with fresh cilantro and a lime wheel.

GLASSWARE
Rocks glass

Grilled Peach Bourbon Sour

SEASON: SPRING & SUMMER

Summertime is grilling time. It's also peach season. The fact that I have a peach tree in the front yard makes this an easy cocktail to keep in rotation for all my summer gatherings. Of course, you don't have to grill the peaches to make this drink shine, as a ripe peach already makes for the juiciest whiskey sour you can have. But grilling takes this stone fruit to another level: The heat intensifies its natural sweetness and adds a subtle charred flavor that accentuates the oak notes of a bourbon. This is a drink that'll have your guests drooling and your neighbors peeking over the fence.

Pineapples and melons are two other fruits that are great to throw on the grill for a variation on this bourbon sour.

INGREDIENTS
- 2 oz bourbon
- 1 oz lemon juice
- ¾ oz honey syrup (see pg. 249)
- 2 grilled peach slices

DIRECTIONS
1. Combine all ingredients in a cocktail shaker and muddle the peach slices. Add ice and shake to chill. Fine strain into a rocks glass over ice.
2. Garnish with an additional grilled peach slice and bouquet of mint.

GLASSWARE
Rocks glass

GRILLED PEACHES
Halve the peaches. Lightly brush with olive oil to keep them from sticking to the grill. Grill on each side on medium heat 4–5 minutes, checking occasionally, until properly charred (don't overcook or the peaches will fall apart). Remove and slice. Set some aside for garnish.

Tea Time

SEASON: SPRING & SUMMER

My love for photography grew alongside my love for home bartending. In the beginning, being able to shoot content for cocktail bars allowed me to sit in on menu development sessions to see how the bar team designed drinks. Keifer Gilbert, a dear friend and amazing bartender, always shared with me his thought process behind why he mixed the ingredients he did. It was at these creative menu sessions that I learned how to create a flavor bomb of a drink by using interesting liqueurs and/or unique syrups to complement any base spirit. This is one of those drinks.

Featuring gin, yellow chartreuse, green tea syrup and orange bitters, this stirred cocktail is the right fit for an elevated night in with friends looking to try new flavors. Tea is one of those common household staples you can use to easily create unique syrups.

Tea syrups truly highlight botanical spirits and herbaceous liqueurs like no other ingredient can.

INGREDIENTS
- 1½ oz gin
- ½ oz yellow chartreuse
- ¼ oz green tea syrup
  (see pg. 248)
- 2-3 dashes orange bitters

DIRECTIONS
1. Combine all ingredients in a mixing glass, add ice and stir to chill. Strain into a rocks glass over ice.
2. Garnish with a lemon twist.

GLASSWARE
Rocks glass

Lady in Blue

SEASON: SPRING & SUMMER

This floral, citrus-forward cocktail blends gin, elderflower, blueberry and lemon. The gin adds a crisp, botanical taste, balancing out the sweetness of the blueberries and elderflower. Bright and beautiful, it makes for the perfect drink to serve for Easter or Mother's Day.

INGREDIENTS
- 2 oz gin
- ½ oz elderflower liqueur
- 1 oz lemon juice
- ½ oz blueberry syrup (see pg. 248)
- 1 egg white

DIRECTIONS
1. Combine all ingredients in a cocktail shaker and shake vigorously without ice. Add ice, then shake to chill. Strain into a chilled coupe glass and express a lemon peel over the top for aroma.
2. Garnish with speared blueberries.

GLASSWARE
Coupe glass

Summer Shandy

SEASON: SPRING & SUMMER

Traditionally, shandies are refreshing, easy-to-make summer drinks consisting of beer and lemonade or citrus soda. This beverage features a little bit of tequila, Campari, fresh grapefruit, lemon and honey syrup, topped off with your choice of pale ale, light lager or wheat beer. Crisp, refreshing, hoppy and slightly bitter, it's my go-to cocktail for converting my lager-loving friends when they think all they want is a brewski. Remember: Summer is a state of mind.

INGREDIENTS
- 1 oz blanco tequila
- ½ oz Campari
- 1 oz grapefruit
- ½ oz lemon
- ½ oz honey syrup
- 2 oz pale ale, light lager or wheat beer

DIRECTIONS
1. Combine first 5 ingredients in a cocktail shaker and shake with ice to chill. Strain into a Collins glass over ice and top with a chilled pale ale, light lager or wheat beer.
2. Garnish with a grapefruit wedge and a bouquet of mint.

GLASSWARE
Collins glass

Heart of Stone

SEASON: SPRING & SUMMER

This drink is a special one. It was created by a good friend of mine, Keifer Gilbert, for a global bartending competition. A pantry of easily accessible ingredients was provided, including orange, lemon, red bell pepper and raspberries, all of which he used to concoct something magical. The drink is different every time you sip. Whether it's the savory notes of the pepper married with the botanical gin base, the acidic tang of the orange juice or the welcome, bold, almost tart sweetness of the raspberry, this bevvy's got all of the flavor points you want to hit in a drink. It can trick you because it reads like a tiki drink but doesn't sip that way. It's made with stuff you can find pretty much year-round at your local grocery store but still tastes exotic. Full of contradictions, and despite the name, this drink has a lot of life.

If you don't already own a juicer, I recommend investing in one. Being able to easily extract fresh juice to use in cocktails and homemade syrups leads to the most flavorful drinks.

INGREDIENTS
- 2 oz gin
- 1 oz red bell pepper juice
- ¾ oz lemon juice
- ¾ oz orange juice
- ¾ oz rich simple syrup
- 3 raspberries

DIRECTIONS
1. Combine all ingredients in a cocktail shaker and muddle the raspberries. Add ice and shake to chill. Fine strain into a Collins glass with crushed or pebble ice.
2. Garnish with raspberries and a bouquet of mint.

GLASSWARE
Collins glass

The King's Shilling

SEASON: SPRING & SUMMER

Bourbon, aged rum, pineapple and coffee make for one of the best cocktails I've had to date. This spirit-forward sipper was created by Sean Traynor, a fantastic drink maker and bar owner based in Phoenix whom I met early in my Apartment Bartender journey. He was working at a cocktail bar named Counter Intuitive, known for its rotating menu concepts, flavorful drinks and boozy sippers. This drink quickly became my go-to whenever I stepped foot in the bar. Coffee and pineapple might seem like an unusual combination, but the pairing is why you'll be sipping more and more while wondering why this drink is so damn good.

INGREDIENTS
- 1 oz bourbon
- 1 oz aged rum
- ¼ oz coffee liqueur
- ¼ oz pineapple syrup (see pg. 249)
- 2–3 dashes aromatic bitters

DIRECTIONS
1. Combine all ingredients in a mixing glass, add ice and stir to chill. Strain into a rocks glass over ice.
2. Garnish with an orange twist and pineapple frond.

GLASSWARE
Rocks glass

Very Berry Punch

SEASON: SPRING & SUMMER

This punch is great for any summer get-together, especially for Memorial Day or the Fourth of July. Prepping a punch bowl is the best way to serve your guests and still have time to enjoy the party (I lean toward larger format cocktails when serving six or more people). This summer punch bowl is fruity, citrus-forward and a stunning bubbly centerpiece to enjoy with good friends and fireworks.

YIELD
About 6 drinks

INGREDIENTS
- 3 cups light rum
- 1½ cups berry syrup (see pg. 248)
- 1½ cups fresh lime juice
- 15-20 dashes orange bitters
- 1 bottle sparkling wine (brut champagne or prosecco)

DIRECTIONS
1. Combine the first 4 ingredients in a pitcher or punch bowl over ice and stir. Add a handful of fresh strawberries and blueberries to the bowl for garnish.
2. Add the sparkling wine just before your guests arrive to avoid it going flat. Serve in a rocks glass over ice and garnish with sliced strawberries and blueberries.

GLASSWARE
Rocks glass

Zonie Land

SEASON: SPRING & SUMMER

Served in a tiki mug, this drink combines a hint of citrus, a bite of chile and the lingering flavor of smoky whiskey. The name is a nod to my early years in Arizona—in college, my friends referred to the Grand Canyon State as Zonie Land. The cocktail originally incorporated a mesquite smoked whiskey, but any peated or smoky whiskey is great.

For more oomph, float ½ oz of an overproof aged rum like Plantation O.F.T.D.

INGREDIENTS
- 2 oz smoky whiskey (I recommend a peated scotch like Laphroaig or Bruichladdich)
- ½ oz chile liqueur (I recommend Ancho Reyes)
- 1 oz pineapple juice
- ½ oz lime juice
- ½ oz orgeat (almond syrup)

DIRECTIONS
1. Combine all ingredients in a cocktail shaker and shake with ice. Strain into a tiki mug (or Collins glass) and top with crushed or pebble ice.
2. Garnish with a bouquet of mint, pineapple fronds and freshly grated nutmeg.

GLASSWARE
Tiki mug or Collins glass

Watermelon Crush

SEASON: SPRING & SUMMER

Put that watermelon from your cookout to good use by throwing it in a vibrant, bubbly cocktail perfect for warm nights. Elderflower liqueurs like St-Germain are commonly referred to as "bartender's ketchup" for their ability to make any drink taste good. The fresh watermelon juice makes this cocktail pop, but the addition of elderflower liqueur adds an aromatic floral flavor that further elevates it.

INGREDIENTS
- 1½   oz gin
- ½   oz elderflower liqueur
- 1½   oz watermelon juice
- ½   oz lime juice
- ½   oz simple syrup
- 1   oz soda water

DIRECTIONS
1. Combine the first 5 ingredients in a cocktail shaker and shake with ice. Fine strain into a wine glass over ice and top with soda water.
2. Garnish with mint and a watermelon slice.

GLASSWARE
Wine glass

Iced Bourbon
Chai Latte

SEASON: FALL & WINTER

The espresso martini isn't the only delectable coffee/liquor cocktail combo out there. When you want to combine the pep and flavor from your first drink of the day with the delicious kick of a late night cocktail, look no further than this boozed-up latte featuring a welcome dash of warming spice courtesy of the chai syrup.

INGREDIENTS
- 1½ oz bourbon (or vodka)
- 2 oz espresso
- ¾ oz chai syrup (see pg. 248)
- Cold-frothed milk

DIRECTIONS
1. Combine the first 3 ingredients in a Collins glass and top with crushed or pebble ice. Lightly stir to combine.
2. Top with a layer of cold-frothed milk or your favorite non-dairy substitute and garnish with a few coffee beans.

GLASSWARE
Collins glass

SEASONAL &
SIGNATURE

Lovebird

SEASON: FALL & WINTER

A beautiful cocktail fit for lovers (or loners). A grape-based spirit, cognac pairs well with the fresh lemon and fruity notes of raspberry syrup and adds a delicate base to this drink. I recommend using a VS (very special) expression of cognac because it's the least aged of cognacs and has a fruity and relatively light flavor profile. The silky mouthfeel of the egg white adds elegance to the drink. This is one I'd mix up for a Valentine's Day dinner.

INGREDIENTS
- 2 oz VS cognac
- 1 oz lemon juice
- ¾ oz raspberry syrup (see pg. 249)
- 2 dashes orange bitters
- 1 egg white

DIRECTIONS
1. Combine all ingredients in a cocktail shaker and shake vigorously without ice. Add ice and shake to chill. Fine strain into a rocks glass with a large cube of ice and express a lemon peel over the top for aromatics.
2. Garnish with dried rose petals.

GLASSWARE
Rocks glass

210 LET'S DO DRINKS

Pomegranate Tequila Tonic

SEASON: FALL & WINTER

I love serving this drink during any fall or winter get-together for the ease, flavor and beautiful color that pomegranate contributes. The warm vanilla and cinnamon notes from the reposado tequila pair perfectly with the sweet-tart flavor of pomegranate juice, which is in peak season during fall and early winter. Reposado tequila is one of my favorite spirits to experiment with, but feel free to use a gin, whiskey or vodka. Whichever way you go, this drink never disappoints.

INGREDIENTS
- 2 oz reposado tequila
- 1 oz pomegranate juice
- ½ oz lemon juice
- ½ oz agave nectar
- 2 dashes aromatic bitters
- 2 oz tonic water

DIRECTIONS
1. Combine the first 5 ingredients in a cocktail shaker and shake with ice. Strain into a highball glass over ice and top with tonic water.
2. Garnish with a sprig of thyme and a lemon slice.

GLASSWARE
Highball glass

Trois Jours
à Cognac
(Three Days in Cognac)

SEASON: FALL & WINTER

It took just three days for me to fall in love with the spirit of Cognac. I visited the region in 2018 and had a chance to stroll through the vineyards, learn about the production process and sip *eau de vie* (distilled unaged brandy) fresh from the still. Cognac adds so much flavor and depth to any cocktail, especially a spirit-forward drink like an old fashioned. It lends a softer touch to an old fashioned than whiskey, so if you like the classic be sure to give this change-up a try. If I could only imbibe one drink for the rest of my life, it'd be a Cognac old fashioned, hands down.

INGREDIENTS
- 2 oz VSOP Cognac
- ¼ oz organic maple syrup
- 2 dashes aromatic bitters
- 2-3 dashes chocolate bitters

DIRECTIONS
1. Combine all ingredients in a mixing glass, add ice and stir to chill. Strain into a rocks glass over ice.
2. Garnish with a lemon twist.

GLASSWARE
Rocks glass

Añejo Nightcap

SEASON: FALL & WINTER

Cinnamon is a personal favorite during the fall and winter months. This warm, sweet and light spice pairs well with añejo tequila and orange liqueur (for a richer flavor I prefer Grand Marnier to Cointreau). Añejo tequilas typically spend one to three years aging in a barrel, often resulting in a smooth taste that can take the place of any great aged spirit. Grand Marnier is also a digestif (post-meal sipper), so these two ingredients in combination make for a great nightcap after a Friendsgiving feast.

Swap out añejo tequila for 1 oz reposado tequila and ½ oz mezcal for a variation on a modern classic: the Oaxacan old fashioned.

INGREDIENTS
- 1½ oz añejo tequila
- ½ oz orange liqueur
- ¼ oz cinnamon syrup (see pg. 248)
- 2 dashes orange bitters
- 2 dashes aromatic bitters

DIRECTIONS
1. Combine all ingredients in a mixing glass, add ice and stir to chill. Strain into a rocks glass over ice.
2. Garnish with a flamed orange peel.

GLASSWARE
Rocks glass

Velvet Apple

SEASON: FALL & WINTER

Apple is a quintessential fall flavor. Apple brandy, grenadine (pomegranate syrup), fresh lemon and egg white come together to create a fruity, tart and citrus-forward drink with a lovely velvety texture. Calvados is my favorite to use in this drink. It's a type of apple brandy named after its region in Normandy, France. It brings such character to an otherwise simple drink with beautiful notes of apple, pear, apricot and baking spices. This makes the perfect pairing for any fall gathering.

INGREDIENTS

- 2 oz apple brandy (I recommend Calvados or applejack)
- ¾ oz grenadine
- 1 oz lemon juice
- 2–3 dashes chocolate bitters
- 1 egg white

DIRECTIONS

1. Combine all ingredients in a cocktail shaker and shake vigorously without ice. Add ice and shake until chilled. Fine strain into a coupe glass.
2. Express a lemon peel over the top of the drink for aromatics. Wrap the twist around a sprig of rosemary, and place on top of the drink. Lightly torch the rosemary sprig for added aroma (optional).

GLASSWARE

Coupe glass

Bourbon Cider

SEASON: FALL & WINTER

Cider during the holidays is a ritual. I make this every year, both for the warmth it provides and the scent of apples and spices it leaves lingering throughout the house. It's a relatively simple process and makes for a great non-alcoholic beverage the whole family can enjoy. Be sure to use a variety of apples ranging in flavor from sweet to tart. Gala, Granny Smith, Golden Delicious and Fuji are some of the best. Add your favorite aged spirit to it and you've got a delicious drink to sip fireside, ensuring you'll feel toasty inside and out.

YIELD
About 6–8 drinks

INGREDIENTS
10–12	apples, sliced
5	whole cinnamon sticks
2–3	whole star anise
3	whole cloves
1	whole nutmeg
2	whole allspice
1	whole orange, cut into slices
½	cup brown sugar (add more to your liking)

DIRECTIONS
1. In a large pot (or large slow cooker), combine all ingredients. For the nutmeg, grate some into the pot before dropping in the whole nutmeg). Cover the mixture with water and bring it to a simmer on medium heat.
2. Reduce to low heat and let cook 1 hour until apples are soft. Lightly mash the apples and continue on low heat for 30 more minutes. (Using a slow cooker may take up to 3 hours.) To store: Allow to cool, then strain through a large fine mesh strainer or cheesecloth to remove the solids. Refrigerate up to 2 weeks.
3. Optional: In a glass mug, add 1½ oz bourbon then top with cider. Garnish with a cinnamon stick and lemon wheel.

GLASSWARE
Glass mug

Good Things
Take Thyme

SEASON: FALL & WINTER

B lood orange season typically starts in December and lasts through winter. In terms of flavor, it isn't very different from a regular navel orange, but the maroon color it lends to a drink is stunning. This is a simple drink I like to make as a welcome cocktail for any winter gathering or holiday party. The orange and vanilla combination make this drink taste like a boozy creamsicle with a bright herbal aroma courtesy of the thyme.

INGREDIENTS
- 2 oz vodka or gin
- 1½ oz blood orange juice
- ¾ oz vanilla syrup (see pg. 249)
- 2–3 dashes orange bitters
- Splash of soda water

DIRECTIONS
1. Combine the first 3 ingredients in a cocktail shaker, add ice and shake to chill. Strain into a snifter and top with a splash of soda water. Add crushed or pebble ice.
2. Garnish with a sprig of thyme and a slice of blood orange.

GLASSWARE
Snifter glass

The Count of Montenegro

SEASON: FALL & WINTER

A drink fit for a noble, this variation on a reverse Manhattan features a personal favorite, Amaro Montenegro. It's the first bottle I reach for when introducing someone to the world of amari. The taste is initially sweet, with flavor profiles of cinnamon, orange and honey, followed by a subtle bitterness. The spice of rye whiskey balances it out—I recommend using an overproof rye. Amaro Montenegro is traditionally served as a digestif, which makes this drink particularly great after a decadent meal—looking at you, Thanksgiving.

For other unique flavor combinations, swap out Montenegro for your favorite amaro like Averna, Nonnino, Cynar or CioCiaro.

INGREDIENTS
- 2 oz Amaro Montenegro
- 1 oz rye whiskey
- 3-4 dashes orange bitters

DIRECTIONS
1. Combine all ingredients in a mixing glass and stir with ice to chill. Strain into a coupe glass.
2. Garnish with an orange slice.

GLASSWARE
Coupe glass

Bananas Foster

SEASON: FALL & WINTER

Bananas Foster has been one of my favorite fall and winter desserts since I was a kid. Now that I'm an adult, I'd rather drink it. This rich, spirit-forward sipper has all the tasting notes of banana, brown sugar, cinnamon, caramel, walnut and chocolate. It's quite literally dessert in a glass. I like to use a 100 proof bourbon to balance out the sweet. For the banana liqueur, a little bit goes a long way. Tempus Fugit and Giffard are two brands that make an incredible range of liqueurs, especially banana. I use Giffard but either would be an amazing addition to both your drink and home bar. Since this cocktail is a bit on the decadent side, you might as well take this drink a step further by garnishing it with a brûléed banana slice. This is a great way to emphasize the banana and impart even more flavor with each sip.

To make brûléed banana, cut a few round slices of banana and sprinkle some brown sugar on top. Using a small culinary torch, lightly wave the flame over the banana to caramelize the sugar for a crunchy texture.

INGREDIENTS
- 2 oz bourbon or rye whiskey
- ¼ oz banana liqueur
- ¼ oz brown sugar syrup (see pg. 248)
- 2–3 dashes black walnut bitters

DIRECTIONS
1. Combine all ingredients in a mixing glass and stir with ice to chill. Strain into a rocks glass over ice.
2. Garnish with freshly grated nutmeg and a brûléed slice of banana.

GLASSWARE
Rocks glass

Earl Grey Negroni

SEASON: FALL & WINTER

Earl Grey is one of the most recognized teas in the world. This beloved black tea is flavored with oil from the rind of bergamot orange, a winter citrus that could also pass as a lemon or lime. The infused gin in this negroni pairs floral notes with the herbal sweetness of sweet vermouth, and the overall flavor is brightened by the citrus notes of Aperol. This drink is a conversation starter, and a great one to batch ahead of a large gathering.

To make the Earl Grey-infused gin, in a pitcher add 1 bottle of gin and 3 high quality Earl Grey tea bags. Let the tea steep for a maximum of 1 hour—any longer may cause the gin to extract too many tannins from the tea, leading to a bitter flavor. Remove and discard the tea bags.

INGREDIENTS

1 oz Earl Grey-infused gin
1 oz Aperol
1 oz sweet vermouth

DIRECTIONS

1. Combine 1 oz Earl Grey-infused gin with Aperol and vermouth in a mixing glass. Add ice and stir to chill. Strain into a rocks glass over ice.
2. Garnish with a lemon twist.

GLASSWARE

Rocks glass

Sparkling Cranberry Cider

SEASON: FALL & WINTER

This cider is a crisp, refreshing combination of apple and cranberry, two fall staples. Add some bubbles and you have a seasonal, celebratory drink perfect for a night with good friends and great food. This is also a great welcome drink for any holiday party with its subtle sweetness and dry finish to ready your palate for a decadent spread. To really make this drink shine, I recommend apple brandy or Calvados as the base spirit to further highlight the apple flavor notes, but bourbon, vodka and gin are all great alternatives.

INGREDIENTS
- 1½ oz Calvados or apple brandy
- 1 oz unsweetened cranberry juice
- ½ oz lemon juice
- 4 oz sparkling apple cider (I recommend Martinelli's Sparkling Cider)

DIRECTIONS
1. Combine all ingredients in a wine glass over ice and lightly stir to combine.
2. Garnish with a sprig of rosemary and a few cranberries.

GLASSWARE
Wine glass

Masala Chai Sour

SEASON: FALL & WINTER

This beautiful citrus-forward cocktail showcases rum, fresh lemon and homemade chai syrup. I love this drink for the pop of winter spices in every sip: vanilla, cinnamon, star anise, clove, allspice and cardamom. The red wine float (I recommend syrah, pinot noir or tempranillo) ties it all together and really makes it stand out visually. When used appropriately, wine can elevate a cocktail in flavor and appearance. It's satisying to hear your guests say "Wow!" when you hand them a drink, and this one will earn that reaction.

INGREDIENTS
- 2 oz aged dark rum
- 1 oz lemon juice
- ¾ oz chai syrup (see pg. 248)
- 1 oz dry red wine

DIRECTIONS
1. Combine the first 3 ingredients in a cocktail shaker. Add ice and shake to chill. Strain into a rocks glass over ice. Lightly pour the dry red wine over the back of a bar spoon to layer on top.
2. Garnish with a star anise.

GLASSWARE
Rocks glass

Carajillo

SEASON: FALL & WINTER

One of the first international work trips I took for Apartment Bartender was to Cartagena, Spain, for Licor 43. It's Spain's most popular liqueur, boasting a flavor profile of vanilla, citrus and other winter spices that make it perfect for the colder months. The Spanish equivalent to an Irish coffee, a carajillo has two ingredients: liquor—in this case, Licor 43—and freshly brewed espresso. It's a simple evening pick-me-up for coffee lovers like me who are always looking for a post-dinner espresso but still want to wind down a little.

INGREDIENTS
1½ oz Licor 43
1 shot freshly brewed espresso

DIRECTIONS
1. In a rocks glass filled with ice, add the Licor 43. Add the espresso shot and lightly stir to combine.
2. Garnish with coffee beans.

GLASSWARE
Rocks glass or a snifter with ice

Red Wine Julep

SEASON: FALL & WINTER

Rather than pouring unfinished bottles of red wine down the drain, as long as it's been open for less than a week, I love to turn leftover vino into syrup. And by adding classic seasonal spices such as cinnamon, star anise, orange peel and allspice, you can elevate the sweet-tart flavor of red wine syrup to make it taste like a sweet mulled wine. The syrup adds a complex flavor and a beautiful hue to any cocktail. Using it in a julep-style cocktail is one of my favorite ways to showcase its complexity.

Spiced red wine syrup is also great in an old fashioned, Sazerac, sidecar, daiquiri, Tom Collins or whiskey sour.

INGREDIENTS
- 1½ oz VSOP cognac
- 1 oz rye whiskey
- ½ oz spiced red wine syrup (see pg. 249)
- 2-3 dashes orange bitters

DIRECTIONS
1. Combine all ingredients in a rocks glass or julep cup and top with crushed or pebble ice. Lightly stir to combine, then top with more ice.
2. Slap a bouquet of sage leaves on your hand to open up the aroma, then garnish the drink with the leaves.

GLASSWARE
Rocks glass or julep cup

Ruby Spice Daiquiri

SEASON: FALL & WINTER

Once I got into cocktails, I was very enthusiastic about showing off my home bartending skills when friends came over. I'd mix everyone their own special drink so that by the time I was done with one, someone was coming back for a refill. I quickly found myself spending way more time behind the counter and not enough time enjoying the gathering. The daiquiri became an easy drink to shake up (or batch beforehand) and pour so I could still enjoy myself. This drink, a play on the Hemingway daiquiri, features rum, grapefruit, lime and cinnamon syrup. You can also scale up the recipe into a winter-centric punch by multiplying the individual recipe measurements by how many drinks you're looking to serve. Combine it all into a punch bowl or pitcher with ice, and it's ready to go. After all, what's the point of throwing a party if you're not enjoying it too?

INGREDIENTS
- 2 oz aged rum
- 1 oz grapefruit juice
- ½ oz lime juice
- ¾ oz cinnamon syrup
  (see pg. 248)

DIRECTIONS
1. Combine all ingredients in a cocktail shaker, add ice and shake to chill. Strain into a coupe glass.
2. Garnish with a grapefruit twist.

GLASSWARE
Coupe glass

Ginger Toddy

SEASON: FALL & WINTER

This warm and comforting combination of whiskey, lemon, ginger, bitters and hot water creates a delicious take on a classic. It's perfect for cold winter nights or whenever you need a little pick-me-up.

INGREDIENTS
- 2 oz whiskey of your choice
- ½ oz ginger syrup (see pg. 248)
- Juice of half a lemon
- 2 dashes aromatic bitters
- 4 oz hot water

DIRECTIONS
1. Combine all ingredients in a glass mug.
2. Garnish with a lemon twist and a piece of candied ginger.

GLASSWARE
Glass mug

Smoke & Ginger

SEASON: FALL & WINTER

Whiskey, ginger, cranberry and chocolate are fall flavors that seem made for each other. Blended Scotch whisky is typically more cocktail-friendly and helps round out the tartness of the cranberry and the spice of the ginger. Chocolate bitters brighten up the flavors to make a cocktail that's just as delicious as it is eye-catching. If you're a fan of Scotch whisky, this is your drink. If you're not yet a fan, consider this your very tasty entry point into a spirit full of history and character.

INGREDIENTS
- 2 oz blended Scotch whisky
- 1 oz unsweetened cranberry juice
- ½ oz lemon
- ¾ oz ginger syrup (see pg. 248)
- 2–3 dashes chocolate bitters
- ½ oz smoky or peated Scotch

DIRECTIONS
1. Combine the first 5 ingredients in a cocktail shaker. Add ice and shake to chill. Strain into a rocks glass over ice and float peated Scotch over the top.
2. Garnish with a lemon twist and candied ginger.

GLASSWARE
Rocks glass

Waffle House

SEASON: FALL & WINTER

grew up on Eggo Waffles, and I still tend to grab a box around the holidays. This cocktail is a riff on the classic flip, with a hint of maple and a hot golden brown waffle on the side to pair. A perfect holiday brunch cocktail for those who like something rich and decadent with a dash of nostalgia.

INGREDIENTS
- 2 oz brandy or bourbon
- 1 whole egg
- ¾ oz organic maple syrup

DIRECTIONS
1. Combine all ingredients in a cocktail shaker without ice and shake to combine. Add ice, then shake to chill. Strain into a coupe glass.
2. Garnish with freshly grated nutmeg and a toasted halved Eggo waffle. Lightly drizzle with maple syrup and serve.

GLASSWARE
Coupe glass

New Year, New Me

SEASON: FALL & WINTER

I never ring in the new year without making a welcome punch for my friends and family. If you're one for the tradition of staying up until midnight on New Year's Eve, consider this a great warm-up drink for the evening. This fruity, spiced sparkling wine-boosted drink incorporates one of my favorite winter liqueurs: St. George Spiced Pear Liqueur. The flavors in this punch pair well with gin, vodka, tequila or rum. Just remember to take it easy so you can enter the new year the right way, sans hangover.

St. George Spiced Pear Liqueur is widely available, but if you can't find it, swap it out for a premium orange liqueur like Grand Marnier or Cointreau.

YIELD
About 6 drinks

INGREDIENTS
- 3 cups gin, vodka, tequila or rum
- 1 cup St. George Spiced Pear Liqueur
- 2 cups fresh grapefruit juice
- 1 cup fresh lime juice
- 1 cup grenadine
- 10–12 dashes Peychaud's bitters
- 1 (750-ml) bottle dry sparkling wine

DIRECTIONS
1. Combine the first 6 ingredients in a punch bowl over ice. Stir to chill and dilute. Add the sparkling wine just before your guests arrive to avoid the bubbles going flat, then add orange wheels, pomegranate seeds and rosemary sprigs for garnish.
2. Serve in a rocks glass over ice.

GLASSWARE
Rocks glass

Homemade Syrup Recipes

Referenced throughout the book, here are some of my favorite syrup recipes you can make in your own kitchen.

BERRY SYRUP

In a medium saucepan on low heat, combine 1 heaping cup sliced strawberries, 1 cup blueberries and 1½ cups water. Bring to a light simmer so the berries begin to split. Gently mash the berries to release the juice. Allow the mix to lightly simmer on low heat. Add 1½ cups sugar and lightly stir to dissolve the sugar. Remove from heat and let cool. Strain out the solids and store the syrup in a sealed glass container in the refrigerator for up to 2 weeks.

BLUEBERRY SYRUP

In a medium saucepan on low heat, combine 1½ cups fresh blueberries and 1 cup water. Bring to a light simmer so the blueberries begin to split. Gently mash the berries to release the juice, and add 1 cup sugar. Lightly stir to dissolve the sugar, then remove from heat and let cool. Strain out the solids and store the syrup in a sealed glass container in the refrigerator for up to 2 weeks.

BROWN SUGAR SYRUP

In a medium saucepan, combine 2 parts brown sugar to 1 part water. Warm on medium-low and lightly stir to dissolve the sugar (do not overheat or bring to a boil). Remove from heat and store in a sealed glass container in the refrigerator for up to 1 month.

CHAI SYRUP

In a small mortar, combine 1 cinnamon stick, 2 to 3 whole allspice, 2 star anise, 2 to 3 cloves, 2 to 3 peppercorns, 2 to 3 coriander seeds, 2 to 3 cardamom pods and 2 to 3 fresh slices of ginger. Crush with a pestle. Lightly toast the spices in a medium saucepan on medium heat for a few minutes before adding 1½ cups water. Bring to a low boil to reduce to 1 cup. Add 1½ cup turbinado sugar and lightly stir to dissolve the sugar. Remove from heat and let cool. Strain out the solids and store the syrup in a sealed glass container in the refrigerator for up to 1 month. For an easier method, use two high quality chai tea bags to 1 cup hot water. Add 1½ cup turbinado sugar and stir to dissolve.

CINNAMON SYRUP

In a medium saucepan on low heat, add 3 broken-up cinnamon sticks and 1 cup water. Bring to a light simmer (do not boil), then add 1 cup sugar. Lightly stir to dissolve the sugar. Remove from heat and let cool. Strain out the solids and store the syrup in a sealed glass container in the refrigerator for up to 2 weeks.

DEMERARA SYRUP

In a medium saucepan, combine 2 parts demerara (or turbinado) sugar to 1 part water. Warm on medium-low heat and lightly stir to dissolve the sugar (do not overheat or bring to a boil). Once the sugar is dissolved, remove from heat and store in a sealed glass container in the refrigerator for up to 1 month.

GINGER SYRUP

In a medium saucepan on low heat, combine equal parts fresh ginger juice and sugar. Lightly stir to dissolve the sugar (do not overheat or bring to a boil). Remove from heat and store in a sealed glass container in the refrigerator for up to 2 weeks.

GREEN TEA SYRUP

In a medium saucepan, bring 1 cup water to a boil. Add 2

bags of green tea (or 2 Tbsp of loose-leaf) and allow the tea to steep. Add 1 cup sugar and lightly stir to dissolve the sugar. Strain out the solids and store the syrup in a sealed glass container in the refrigerator for up to 2 weeks.

HONEY SYRUP

In a medium saucepan, combine 2 parts honey to 1 part water. Warm on medium-low heat and lightly stir to combine the mixture (do not overheat or bring to a boil). Once the honey and water are combined, remove from heat and store in a sealed glass container in the refrigerator for up to 1 month.

LAVENDER SYRUP

In a saucepan on low heat, combine 1½ Tbsp dried lavender and 1 cup water. Bring to a light simmer, then add 1 cup sugar. Lightly stir to dissolve the sugar. Remove from heat and let cool. Strain out the solids and store the syrup in a sealed glass container in the refrigerator for up to 2 weeks.

PASSION FRUIT SYRUP

In a medium saucepan, combine 1 cup water and 1 cup sugar. Halve 4 to 5 passion fruits and scoop the pulp into the saucepan. Warm on medium-low heat and lightly stir to dissolve sugar. Remove from heat and allow it to steep and cool. Strain out the solids and store the syrup in a sealed glass

container in the refrigerator for up to 2 weeks.

PINEAPPLE SYRUP

In a medium saucepan on medium-low heat, combine equal parts pineapple juice and sugar. Lightly stir to dissolve the sugar (do not overheat or bring to a boil). Remove from heat and store in a sealed glass container in the refrigerator for up to 2 weeks.

RASPBERRY SYRUP

In a medium saucepan on low heat, combine 1½ cups fresh raspberries and 1 cup water. Bring to a light simmer so the raspberries begin to split. Gently mash the berries, then add 1 cup sugar. Lightly stir to dissolve the sugar. Remove the syrup from heat and let cool. Strain out the solids and store the syrup in a sealed glass container in the refrigerator for up to 2 weeks.

RICH SIMPLE SYRUP

In a medium saucepan, combine 2 parts sugar to 1 part water. Warm on medium-low heat and lightly stir to dissolve the sugar (do not overheat or bring to a boil). Once the sugar is dissolved, remove from heat and store in a sealed glass container in the refrigerator for up to 1 month.

SIMPLE SYRUP

In a medium saucepan, combine equal parts water and sugar. Warm on medium-

low heat and lightly stir to dissolve the sugar (do not overheat or bring to a boil). Once the sugar is dissolved, remove from heat and store in a sealed glass container in the refrigerator for up to 1 month.

SPICED RED WINE SYRUP

In a saucepan on medium heat, add 1 broken up cinnamon stick, 1 star anise, 2 allspice and 4 to 5 orange peels. Toast the spices for a few minutes before adding 1 cup red wine and the juice from half an orange. Bring the mixture to a light simmer (do not boil), then add 1 cup sugar. Lightly stir to dissolve the sugar. Remove from heat and let cool. Strain out the solids and store the syrup in the refrigerator for up to 1 month.

VANILLA SYRUP

In a medium saucepan, combine 1 part turbinado or white granulated sugar to 1 part water. Add in 1 Tbsp organic pure vanilla extract. Warm on medium-low heat and lightly stir to dissolve the sugar (do not overheat or bring to a boil). Once the sugar is dissolved, remove from heat and let cool. Store in a sealed glass container in the refrigerator for up to 2 weeks.

INDEX

ACKNOWLEDGMENTS

To my mom, who always believed in me and told me as a little boy that I would write a book someday, thank you for being my biggest supporter. To my friends who encouraged me and to all those I've had the privilege of sharing a drink with along the way—thank you for inspiring me to keep going. And to those who use this book to create great moments with your friends and family, cheers to you.

ABOUT THE AUTHOR

ELLIOTT CLARK, also known as Apartment Bartender, is a well-respected tastemaker, influential cocktail creator, spirits writer and content creator. What started out as a hobby of making cocktails at home developed into a successful career that takes Elliott all over the world mixing drinks for some of the world's most notable brands and making the world of spirits more accessible to the at-home cocktail enthusiast.

Media Lab Books
For inquiries, call 646-449-8614

Published by Topix Media Lab
14 Wall Street, Suite 3C
New York, NY 10005

Printed in China

ISBN-13: 978-1-956403-56-5
ISBN-10: 1-956403-56-6

CEO Tony Romando

Vice President & Publisher Phil Sexton
Senior Vice President of Sales & New Markets Tom Mifsud
Vice President of Retail Sales & Logistics Linda Greenblatt
Chief Financial Officer Vandana Patel
Vice President of Manufacturing & Distribution Nancy Puskuldjian
Digital Marketing & Strategy Manager Elyse Gregov

Chief Content Officer Jeff Ashworth
Senior Acquisitions Editor Noreen Henson
Creative Director Susan Dazzo
Photo Director Dave Weiss
Executive Editor Tim Baker
Managing Editor Tara Sherman

Content Editor Juliana Sharaf
Content Designer Mikio Sakai
Features Editor Trevor Courneen
Designer Glen Karpowich
Copy Editor & Fact Checker Madeline Raynor
Junior Designer Alyssa Bredin Quirós
Assistant Photo Editor Jenna Addesso
Assistant Managing Editor Claudia Acevedo

Photography by Elliott Clark and Shawn Campbell
except: Lyndon French: pg. 7; Zoe Rain: pg. 8 (center right), pg. 12 (bottom right);
James Tran: pg. 8 (bottom right); Shawn Campbell: pg. 11; courtesy Hilton Hotels: pg. 255

Indexing by R studio T, NYC

1C-K23-1